# MRS MONEYPENNY
# CRUNCH TIME

COLUMNS FROM THE FINANCIAL TIMES 2008 - 2009

# MRS MONEYPENNY
# CRUNCH TIME

COLUMNS FROM THE FINANCIAL TIMES 2008 - 2009

Masterley Publishing

First published 2009 by
MASTERLEY PUBLISHING

Layout and Artwork: Suzette Field

ISBN: 978-0-9560654-2-1

Printed in the UK by CPI William Clowes Beccles NR34 7TL

*This book is dedicated to Louise Walker, manager and proprietor of Pilot Flight Training, who, as a working mother, entrepreneur and pilot has been such an inspiration to me throughout the recession.*

# INTRODUCTION

"Mummy, what did you do during the credit crunch?" Is a question that the young children of today will be asking in ten to fifteen year's time when we look back at the worst recession since the Second World War. My own children, usually known as cost centres, are older and will already have the answer. Their mother was running a business, buying a house, learning to fly and adjusting to a substantially reduced cash flow. Plus she was sharing all this every week with the readers of the Weekend Financial Times.

When this column first appeared, ten years ago, the cost centres were just sons numbers one, two and three, ageing from one to ten, and their mother was a former pupil of a school in Brighton who worked in a Dutch bank. Ten years later the credit crunch has done for both the school and the bank, but Mrs Moneypenny and indeed the Weekend Financial Times are still going strong.

The recession isn't over yet, I keep telling the cost centres (and anyone else who will listen). But hey, if we can get this much done while it is going on, bring on the recovery!

**Mrs Moneypenny**
*November 2009*

# ACKNOWLEDGEMENTS

This book would never have made it from conception to delivery without the hard work of two people in particular; I am great at ideas but the execution tends to be left trailing behind. Jessica Seldon acted as researcher, editor, and emergency ghost writer for the whole project – for those of you who think it's just a question of copying the columns from the FT website to the page, think again. She deserves a big mention and an even bigger thank you. THANK YOU, Jessica. My publisher Suzette Field at Masterley Publishing is a design whizz, a master project manager and a towerhouse of energy....but then she is another working mother, so that's no surprise.

There are many other people who have made this book possible. Charles Peattie, for instance, famous for drawing the Alex cartoons, did the jacket illustrations. However, the real thank you to him is for standing in every time Mr M decides he is not attending yet another black tie function. Charles, you look fabulous in a dinner jacket.

Finally, my thanks to the Editor of the Financial Times, Lionel Barber, for his support for me even when I throw myself down the stairs in front of him. See page 65.

## PROFIT OF DOOM

*Jan 5, 2008*

Happy New Year. What does 2008 hold for you? I am never confident of predicting anything other than death or taxes, but one thing that I do confidently predict for me this year is that I am going to have to go through a refinancing.

Thankfully we are not talking about a massive writedown of dodgy assets followed by a desperate plea to some or other Sovereign Wealth Fund to buy mandatory convertible stock in Moneypenny Enterprises. It is just that our original facilities, put in place to allow me to lead the buyout of our company, will have run their allotted course and must be replaced. This will involve a pleasant conversation with the bank manager, followed by the submission of our accounts and the exchange of a few legal documents. No, I forgot – we have to find a new bank.

We have been sacked by ours. Why? Not for bad behaviour, I can assure you. We have repaid the vast majority of the debt we amassed to finance the purchase of the company, and have never increased our working capital line even though the business has doubled in size and we have set up a subsidiary business. All investment so far has come from our own resources, through careful cash flow management and incredibly efficient work by our office manager on our receivables.

So you would think that our bank would be pleased to extend the relationship. Not a bit of it.

When we set up our original debt facility, we were delighted to be working with our bank, which, while charging as though it were the Bank of England lending to Northern Rock, did at least get the deal done. After being turned down by five others, the bank that finally said yes appeared to us much as the Government of Singapore Investment Corporation must have appeared to UBS in early December. Here was a partner prepared to back us in our hour of need.

But now we have been told to go elsewhere. We have the whole of 2008 to do so, which is just as well, given the amount of work this will entail and the general credit climate that we will face. Our business has flourished; it has a strong balance

1

sheet and a bright future, and we have talented teams in both the main business and our new offshoot, so I don't predict a round of rejections such as those I received in 2004. But even so, what a pain!

We all know that changing banks – whether personally or corporately – is a nightmare of paperwork, which is why so few of us actually do it.

Our crime is that we are too small, or rather, considering we have doubled in size since we did the original deal, that we need too little money. Our bank has worked out over the past few years that it takes just as much time and effort to process a credit for £5m as £50,000 or £500,000 (funny that), and so it has decided to set £5m as the minimum it will handle. But we don't need a working capital line of £5m and I haven't seen anything for sale that is worth anything like that much. Indeed, having cast an eye over some other companies in our sector, we decided that a start-up made more sense than an acquisition, and doing that cost us a lot less than £5m.

So now we are not a customer of our bank so much as a rounding error. And at some point in 2008 I shall be trudging about explaining our business model and future prospects to a number of banks that are happy to work with a small business.

Actually, I could talk about our business all day, so proud am I of what it does and the people who work for it. But it will take a lot of time, and given that our financial year end is towards the middle of the year, it is likely to coincide with all the things I would rather be doing – the Chelsea Flower Show, Ascot, Wimbledon (I have already been invited to the Final – how efficient is that for invitations?), Henley and the Cartier polo, to name but a few.

How is a girl supposed to get through all that and meet endless bank managers as well? Looks like 2008 is going to be a busy year.

## DOWN TO EARTH
*Jan 12, 2008*
Visiting New York is always appealing. In mid-December I went for 24 hours and managed to make every minute count.

Here's how: fly in late at night and go straight to bed, then
up early to deal with the day's email before sallying forth
into the Manhattan day. An excellent breakfast on my own
in a random café in mid-town reading the FT; three business
meeting, three visits to important shops (including, with express
instructions, The World of Golf); a wander round the Robert
Capa exhibition; then an early dinner and home again, sleeping
overnight on the way back.

It was that easy. Given that the pound now buys two dollars,
it is no wonder that Fifth Avenue is turning into Oxford Street
and three out of four people in all the upmarket stores do not
sound like locals. And what I love about New York at Christmas
time is that they all take it so seriously – even the walk-in nail
bars have extensive decorations, not just around the walls and
ceilings but on each and every nail technician's trolley. Not
that they call it Christmas of course – the US is the home of the
"happy holidays" greeting, one which I can never get used to. (I
never seem to get used to lots of their other expressions, either,
such as "reaching out to". You don't "reach out" to someone.
You call them, or e-mail them, or write to them. So why not say
that?)

What makes such trips a really palatable proposition, as I have
said before, is that I can fly with an airline that has a dedicated
terminal and that – equally important – does not depart from
Heathrow. Just in case I needed reminding of the bliss that it is
to avoid using Heathrow, I flew out of there just after Christmas,
to spend the New Year in the Caribbean.

This was a lot less glamorous than it sounds and Heathrow,
to be fair, was the least of the problems. Virgin Atlantic's
exhortation to cut down on time spent at the airport by
checking-in online proved impossible three times over
– remotely on my computer (the website just refused, even after
half an hour on the phone to Virgin); at the airport's automatic
check-in kiosk ("Sorry, we cannot print at the moment"); and
then even when a helpful assistant took me off to her terminal,
which promptly jammed. So we stood in line for an hour at the
so-called "bag drop" which wasn't functioning as a bag drop at

all, but as an old-fashioned check-in.

By the time Mr M's in-seat entertainment had failed to function in spite of repeated re-setting by the cabin crew, any appearance by Sir Richard Branson would have resulted in my husband being arrested for assault.

We (and that included me) flew to Barbados in economy. As regular readers will know, I firmly believe that children should not fly business class until they can pay for it themselves, and that the under-12s should be banned from the first-class cabin. But even allowing for those strictures, taking a family of five to the Caribbean in peak season is still prohibitively expensive. And thanks to the malfunctioning of the Virgin check-in system we were seated all over the place. Cost Centre #1 ended up in a window seat far away from me, next to a mother/daughter combo that, shall we say, did not strike me as the likeliest dinner companions for him. I occasionally cast a glance in his direction during the flight and, to my concern, saw him flashing his £2,500 of orthodontistry at them, a tactic guaranteed to melt the heart of even the most hard-bitten female.

When I met him later in the queue for the loo, I urged caution – you have to be careful who you smile at in economy. Look at me. I met his father while travelling at the back of the plane. Nineteen years of marriage and three Cost Centres later, and here I am standing in The World of Golf on East 47th Street asking if they stock Titleist NXT Tour balls.

## Way to go

*Feb 02, 2008*

My father turned 80 this week. He continues to drive, work a day a week at the Citizens Advice Bureau, publish the parish magazine from his home computer and attend art classes. I am not sure how long all these things will continue, but I am delighted and encouraged by how active he remains and hope I will be the same at his age.

I will have to be. Now that we are all going to live to 100, I almost expect to be in full-time work at that age – a fate that my father has escaped, having had the wisdom to retire on an index-

linked civil service pension. Considering this, I am reminded
of Alan Greenspan, who retired from running the US Federal
Reserve two years ago, on January 31 2006, just five weeks
short of his 80th birthday. You could argue that he held on a bit
long, but I think he is an example to the rest of us not to give up
too early.

And now we have Sir Winfried Bischoff, appointed to chair
Citigroup at the age of 66. Most people think 66 would be an
acceptable age at which to put one's feet up and have a cup of
tea, especially if you had had as long and successful a career
as Sir Win. But no, why not accept a job chairing one of the
world's biggest banks? And this isn't just a case of showing
up for a few board meetings and hosting the AGM, either.
There's real work to do for the new chairman of Citi – it has
a new chief executive officer and its capital needs shoring up.
Sir Win took over as chairman after Citi had parted company
with the previous incumbent, Chuck Prince, a man nearly 10
years Sir Win's junior who, according to the statement, retired
– yes, retired. Forget 66, the pace of work required at Citi just
now would make most 26-year-olds feel exhausted. I'm all for
it myself. Go, Win! If you follow Alan Greenspan's example,
you've only got another 14 years to go.

The US is much better than Britain at keeping its citizens in
work longer – hence my surprise at Prince's retirement in his
50s. Warren Buffett will turn 78 in August, and shows no signs
of slowing down. And even William Henry Gates III, that bright
young thing that Buffett has enlisted to help him give away his
billions, will turn 53 this October.

Mr M, who is a year younger than Bill Gates, thinks that he
should be allowed to retire now. He regards work as something
that gets in the way of golf. Not that it actually does seem to get
in the way of golf, or at least the pursuit of golfing knowledge.
Tim Yeo, the FT's golf columnist, e-mailed me recently to ask
if I would pass on to Mr M his inquiry about which Australian
golf courses he should play during a forthcoming visit. This
assumed, Tim added, that he managed to get his golf/wife
balance right during the trip. Quite.

I duly forwarded the e-mail and Mr M kindly copied me in on his reply. To my consternation, he displayed a knowledge of Australian golf courses far more extensive than I had anticipated. Not only did he recommend several that I had never heard of, but he described them almost down to the last blade of grass – I was surprised he didn't tell Tim which clubs to use. And by the way, Mr M was able to send his reply from the office during the working day without the need to consult any of the yards of books we have at home (example: *1,001 Golf Holes You Must Play Before You Die*).

No doubt if my father lived in the US he would, like Mr Greenspan, be thinking of retirement only now. Or maybe not – there is one big difference between them. My mother turns 80 this year as well. Mr Greenspan, on the other hand, is married to a woman 20 years his junior. Maybe that's the secret – and I need to start looking for a 25-year-old.

## SUITED AND BOOTED
*Feb 09, 2008*

I was very nervous before going to Davos. No, it was not the thought of rubbing shoulders with more than 1,000 of the world's business and political leaders (and apparently 10,000 support staff). It was about what to wear while doing so.

You would think that being a girl would be an advantage at the World Economic Forum, where again this year only 17 per cent of delegates were female. But it is hard to stand out against the phalanxes of suited men when you can't dress to impress. The most crucial part of a woman's wardrobe – footwear – is not available to her. It's hiking boots, snow boots, or nothing – otherwise you will fall over, or worse, get wet feet as you move from one venue to another.

With the Jimmy Choos firmly in the wardrobe at home there seemed little point in wearing a skirt, so it was trousers for me, although I did notice both Indra Nooyi, CEO of PepsiCo, and HM Queen Rania of Jordan in skirts on stage during one forum. Mind you, it's different for the VIPs (and to be a VIP at Davos you have to be a real VIP as almost everyone there runs a company or a country). They are chauffeured everywhere, so perhaps they didn't need to be quite as careful as us mere mortals forced to travel à pied.

Naturally, I looked at the delegate list before I went and noticed to my delight/horror that Anshu Jain was due to attend. Not that I could get an invite to the Deutsche Bank party, you understand (and I did try the straightforward method of asking for one). My company was good enough for John Thain and Jamie Dimon, but not Josef Ackermann.

Well never mind – maybe I would meet Mr Jain on one of my numerous yomps (in not very glamorous footwear) up and down the Promenade, or while milling around in the Congress Centre, or even while strategically wandering up and down the corridor in the Hotel Belvedere that housed the DB press office. So before leaving for Switzerland I booked myself in for a 10,000 mile service at the beauty therapist and hairdresser, just in case.

I took hand luggage only – spare socks, shirt and knickers, a washbag and a computer – but my overnight bag was not nearly as comprehensively packed as my handbag. As well as the obvious (purse, notebook, pen and business cards) I needed my earmuffs and sunglasses (for when I ventured outside) reading glasses (for poring over the notes in the dimly-lit sessions), gloves, Blackberry, phone, newspaper, make-up …

I did pack the key jewellery and one smart jacket, and thank goodness I did, because the women that did make it to Davos had a world agenda – and when powerful women meet each other, they dress up. Sitting here in our little world of falling stockmarkets and bailed-out banks it is easy to forget that once upon a time, the world set eight Millennium Development Goals that it pledged to achieve by 2015.

Although progress on all of them has not been as fast as it might have been, there has been some movement on all but one – number five, which calls for the maternal mortality rate to fall by three-quarters. Some 530,000 women still die in childbirth each year, as I was reminded at the women-only dinner hosted by Indra Nooyi, Wendi Murdoch and Queen Rania.

Held in the Davos Golf Club (how many of you knew that Davos had a golf club?) it united 40 extraordinary female achievers (and me) and even launched its very own webpage, www.myspace.com/davosdinner. There might not be many women at Davos, but the ones that were there were determined to make themselves count.

Not that it remained women-only for the entire evening. The event took on a somewhat surreal air once the girls had had the call to arms (and you could not listen to our speakers without being moved – even a hardened old cynic like me can be transported to new levels of determination by listening to Ngozi Okonjo-Iweala, joint managing director of the World Bank and the former Nigerian minister of finance).

Suddenly, a white-jacketed waiter looking suspiciously like Bono appeared with a plate of food, followed by that consummate sommelier Rupert Murdoch with the wine refills, and the Google trio of Larry, Sergey and Eric did the water round. How amazing is that? Even in Davos, I doubt there was another event quite like it.

It felt like I had had the whole Davos experience in one go, I reflected on the train to Zurich the next day. The issues of our times, the women who can make things happen, the world's business and political leaders. But not, I realised, even after all my best efforts, Anshu Jain.

Next year, perhaps less money at the hairdresser and more to a charity that can help reduce maternal mortality.

A HEAVY SLEEPER
*Feb 16, 2008*
On January 9 I was unconscious for four hours. No, I had not stood in the way of a golf ball, or taken my boxing training to new levels.

I was knocked out, deliberately, by a consultant anaesthetist in order to have some planned surgery.

Let me assure you that I am fine. But I was concerned about the procedure – not because of the surgery, but because of the anaesthetic. We may be able to map the human genome, but still no one knows precisely how anaesthetics work.

One thing we do know, however, is that if you are fat it takes more to knock you out. The first time I endured the humiliation of being publicly weighed was when I chartered a helicopter to show me and my family around Barbados; they weighed us all to calculate how much fuel was needed. Similarly, my weight determined how much propofol it would take to put me to sleep and keep me that way. (You can imagine that since higher Body Mass Index = higher dosage, I required industrial quantities to get the job done.)

Propofol has been around for about 25 years and has in effect taken over from all other intravenous anaesthetics in the developed world. It has significant advantages over anaesthesia using gas, a technique invented about 150 years ago. However, it lowers the blood pressure in almost everyone (me included) and there is some evidence that, in extreme cases, this can affect how well patients fare after surgery.

As with all general anaesthetics, we do not understand precisely how propofol does its work. Doctors now believe that anaesthetic drugs act on specific "receptors" – groups of molecules that are made by cells and inserted into their surface. In the brain, the anaesthetic binds to its receptor and causes changes in the way the cell functions. These changes, occurring in many cells, result in unconsciousness.

Giving a patient too much anaesthetic is expensive and delays recovery. Yet even though there is a good chance that genetic make-up is as important as weight in determining dosage, no one has worked out how to link one to the other.

At least, not yet. I had an anaesthetist who wasn't just handsome and clever but happened to be studying this very question. So great was my fascination with the entire process ("Why are you putting me under? Can't we talk about this some more?" and so on) that he probably speeded up simply to shut me up. Hopefully, by the end of his study he will be able to suggest more accurate methods of determining the dose than just putting me on the scales.

It looks, on the surface, very promising. At St Thomas'

Hospital, where my consultant works, he has studied hundreds of surgical patients. But there are two problems. The first is that he has no one to help him. Research into anaesthesia at St Thomas', the preserve of the University of London, declined sharply a few years ago when the professor of anaesthetics retired and the academic department was shut. The second is that he has no funding. Despite prostituting himself by working privately on Wednesdays putting overweight middle-aged women (and others) to sleep, he won't be able to afford to pay for the genetic analysis of hundreds of blood samples.

Given that the world market for propofol, estimated at $700m in 2006, is growing by 15 to 20 per cent a year, and that even minor improvements in its side-effect profile have potential commercial significance, I am astonished that no one wants to fund his work.

My tolerance of pain is minimal – I practically need an anaesthetic to have my legs waxed – so I was delighted that my consultant also pumped me full of morphine. When I went home, I made him write up for me virtually the whole of the British National Formulary for my pain relief. My take-home drugs were not covered by my medical insurance, and as I parted with the cash I wondered why drug manufacturers don't use some of their profits to pay for his research. They are not likely to run out of money – after all, I'm not the only person in the world not as thin as she should be, and so the profits from propofol are likely to continue flowing. But surely the first manufacturer to offer a formulation allowing people with the right genes to take smaller doses will be able to command an even bigger premium. Or in my post-operative haze, am I missing something?

## ALARMS AND EXCURSIONS
*Mar 01, 2008*
I have never been a cigarette smoker. Come to that, I've never been a smoker of anything. I got through school and university without taking it up and after that the idea seemed rather pointless. Mr M, too, has never smoked - as a fanatical

Australian sportsman he eschewed cigarettes in favour of greater lung capacity, and believed smoking was a pastime only for the foolish.

The foolish, it turns out, include his eldest son. Cost Centre #1 outed himself as a ''social smoker'' a little while ago. We immediately enforced a 25 per cent cut in his allowance and made it abundantly clear that we wished him to give up. To no avail - I resigned myself to having a smoker in the family and resolved to try harder with CC#2.

But then we had An Incident. One Monday evening CC#1 called me at 10.25pm to inform me that he was about to be carpeted by his housemaster. Why? Because he had been smoking in his room and had set off the fire alarm. My immediate thought was ''how stupid can you get?,'' followed swiftly by a note to self to marry further up the gene pool before having any more children. I am not surprised that the school took a dim view - apart from being a fire hazard, his actions had forced the evacuation into the freezing night of 60 teenage boys, some of whom had flu.

He was not suspended. (I have always been amazed that suspension is seen as a punishment. Whose punishment? If they send him home I will have to deal with him, and the punishment will be more mine than his. I will be completely stressed, while he will be enjoying a well-stocked fridge and 200-plus television channels.) However, he was saved from suspension because he is directing and starring in a house production of 12 Angry Men, and his housemaster would make it 13 if he was not around for rehearsals. Instead, CC#1 was confined to the library for five days during all non-lesson time. Now that's what I call a punishment.

A week later, he came home to change on his way to an 18th birthday party.

He had, he said, given up smoking. He had been to the doctor and had been given a prescription for nicotine chewing gum. This is provided by the National Health Service. I applauded his initiative, but did wonder if it was a good use of taxpayers' money. You can buy it over the counter in pharmacies, after all.

He reported back after the party that he had managed to stay off the cigarettes. However, it emerged that this victory had been won at some cost. He informed me gravely that he would have to rethink his social strategies. Two of them - excusing himself from a boring conversation to go and have a cigarette, and offering to take a girl outside for a cigarette in order to be with her alone - were no longer open to him.

Meanwhile CC#2 has been practising his social strategies - in French. He has been demanding for some time that he be sent on a course to improve his spoken French. In response to his cri de coeur, I found a nice couple, both teachers, living near Montpelier who take in children aged 12-18 in small groups. They give them a week's language practice by rehearsing vocabulary every day and then using it at the shops, in the kitchen and on various outings. CC#2 took along his school books and some practice Common Entrance papers and had a great time, not least because his teachers fixed up three separate visits to meet local children. By day three even his text messages were in French.

CC#1 abandoned the study of French when he was 16, two years ago. He abandoned the use of cigarettes only two weeks ago. He called yesterday to report that a further unexpected by-product of his decision to quit was that he had found he suddenly had at least an hour a day spare. What, I asked, had this time been used for? Diligent studying of his academic subjects, like his brother? ''Mother,'' he replied, ''now it is you being foolish.''

## A PLACE FIT FOR HEROES
*Mar 08, 2008*

In the first half of the 19th century, there raged in the newspapers of the day a great public debate. A military hero, long dead, remained – shamefully – uncommemorated. Money for a memorial was readily available, without troubling the public purse, having been raised by public subscription from those who appreciated his contribution to saving England from defeat by the French.

A statue was eventually commissioned, but even then that was not the end of the matter. There remained the vexed question of where it should stand. Trafalgar Square was proposed, but such was the resistance from a number of prominent people that the question was considered by parliament. After the matter went to a vote Trafalgar Square won the day and up went the statue of Horatio Nelson.

But fast forward to 2008. A military hero, long dead, remains – shamefully – uncommemorated. Money for a memorial is readily available, without troubling the public purse, because it has been raised from a successful businessman. That businessman is also a military historian who appreciates the contribution that this individual made to saving England (and particularly London) from, in this case, the Nazis.

A statue has been commissioned from a leading New Zealand sculptor, an appropriate choice since the long-dead hero was of New Zealand origin.

But there remains the vexed question of where the statue is to be sited. Trafalgar Square has been proposed, but there is some resistance. And this time the debate cannot be considered by parliament because the Mayor of London now has authority over Trafalgar Square.

Regular readers of this column will know that the sadly ignored hero I refer to is Royal Air Force officer Sir Keith Park. In February 1947 Lord Tedder, Chief of the Air Staff, said of him: "If any one man won the Battle of Britain, he did. I do not believe it is realised how much that one man, with his leadership, his calm judgement and his skill, did to save, not only this country, but the world."

The obvious site for a memorial to Sir Keith is the fourth plinth in Trafalgar Square, within sight of the New Zealand High Commission and alongside other military heroes to whom we owe so much, including Nelson. But the Mayor of London, Ken Livingstone, has delegated the decision over what will occupy the fourth plinth to the Fourth Plinth Commissioners, who have initiated a programme of contemporary art commissions. The next commission, from a shortlist of six, will be announced this spring. I have nothing against modern art (even if I don't understand much of it), but I do believe there are more appropriate places for it in London than Trafalgar Square.

On Friday, RAF representatives and RAF veterans of the Battle of Britain, gathered in Trafalgar Square, alongside a full-size replica Spitfire, to launch a campaign to persuade the commissioners that a memorial to Sir Keith would be so much more appropriate. I urge all of you, and not just Londoners, to visit the campaign website www.sirkeithpark.com to see how you can help.

Those of us who live in London have a separate opportunity to make our voices heard, because a Mayoral election will be held on May 1.

So here are a few facts that everyone, London voters especially, might wish to consider. All of the pieces being considered by the Fourth Plinth Commissioners will cost London taxpayers a considerable sum.

The statue of Sir Keith Park will cost them nothing.

Trafalgar Square is a national public space of such significance that Hitler had planned to remove its contents to Germany had Operation Sealion, his invasion plan, succeeded. The square has several memorials for the navy and the army, but not one for the Royal Air Force. And there is no memorial of any note to Sir Keith Park in the city that he did so much to save.

There are still people who remember Sir Keith. Let us act while they are still with us. I would like to think that in 2010, the 70th anniversary of the Battle of Britain, I could take my children and show them the statue of Sir Keith Park, standing next to that of Horatio Nelson. For without the former, the latter would almost certainly no longer be there.

## MIND THE GAPS
*Mar 14, 2008*

What have you forgotten recently? I was stood up for breakfast the other day because someone who had fixed a date with me a month ago forgot they had done so. No matter, these things

14

happen, I don't take it personally, I said when she called to apologise. But she might find it challenging to get a date in my diary for a while.

One thing I did not forget this year was Valentine's Day. I got up at 6am to write a card to Mr M before getting him out of bed to take me to the station, sneaking it on to his pillow to find when he returned. Mr M however just about managed a grunt, but nothing else, when I got out of the car. Then he must have gone home, read the Australian newspapers online and realised what date it was, for halfway to London I got a very apologetic e-mail. He claimed he had bought me a card, written it, put it in his bag and forgotten it. Isn't that a typical man?

Later on he found the card I had left on his pillow, and an even more apologetic e-mail arrived. By then he must have realised he was in serious trouble, so I was not surprised when a beautiful bunch of white roses arrived at my office. I e-mailed my thanks, also telling him that all was forgiven. Alas, Mr M's reply revealed that the flowers were not from him.

So now I have a secret admirer. I am all for secret admirers – they're just what a woman needs when she is fast approaching 46 and feeling fat. Of course, I tried calling the florist to find out who had sent them. "Sorry luv," she said, "they were booked through Interflora so I've no idea."

We shall just have to hope that Mr M remembers our 20th wedding anniversary in December. I'm afraid, though, that I hold out little hope.

I have long suspected that he might not have the sharpest memory for anything other than sports statistics. Want to know how many left-handed batsmen have scored a century for Australia in Test cricket since the Second World War? And all of their names? He's your man. Sadly, however, that question does not feature on the application for British citizenship form, which he has recently been completing.

Part of the form inquires if the applicant has been married before. Mr M, as some of you may remember, had a starter marriage – to a dentist – before taking me on. When we moved to Hong Kong, in 1994, we signed up to a practice run by a dentist who had qualified at Guy's Hospital in London in the same year as the First Mrs M.

As I was lying horizontal in the surgery one day, looking at the wall of certificates, I asked if this dentist had known her. "Yes," he said, "But I haven't seen her for a few years, since she married some sports-mad Australian. I went to their wedding, actually." I went straight home and asked Mr M if our dentist looked familiar. Mr M said it was completely unreasonable of me to expect him to remember everyone who had been at his wedding.

He had a point. The first question on the application form concerning his previous marriage asked for the name of FMM. Not only could Mr M not remember her middle name, but he didn't know whether her surname had an "e" on the end of it or not. Then he was completely unable to remember her date of birth – guesses ranged between February and October, he was reasonably sure it was 1957, but as for the actual date, not a chance. Finally, the form asked for the date of his marriage. "Ah," he said, "I know that – it was the day of the Wimbledon ladies' final." Great. I shall have to call the All England Lawn Tennis Club before we can complete the form.

I put it to Mr M that it seemed a little harsh to forget quite so much about someone who had once meant so much to him. If I left him tomorrow, would he immediately forget my name, my birthday and the date of our marriage? He pointed out that his starter marriage had been more than 20 years ago, and that if I left him tomorrow, he would be past 70 by the time 20 years had elapsed. "And by then," he said, "I'm sure I'll be forgetting all sorts of things."

## READ MY LIPS
*Mar 22, 2008*

I am not a literature buff. My reading largely consists of *The Economist* and historical biography, and I rarely pick up a novel other than when I'm on holiday. I differ in this regard from many of The Girlfriends. Most Glamorous Girlfriend, for example, read English Literature at Bristol University and can quote Jane Austen – and more obscure authors – at length.

My Teaching Girlfriend, whose specialist subject is English, is also a great lover of literature though she has difficulty with cookery books. Unlike MGG, who can turn things out exactly as they appear in the photographs, TG struggles to move from concept to actuality with her dinner party offerings. Personally, I believe it is utter madness for any wife and mother who works full time to be throwing mid-week dinner parties one has cooked oneself. If it were me, and even if I were on a teacher's salary, I would buy in from M&S or even ask the guests to show up with a course each.

But TG is the right side of 40 and still has that naive, youthful approach to life that involves trying to be the perfect hostess. So as well as being able to recite T.S. Eliot, she is also raising two children and is deputy headmistress of a girls' school. She recently held a mid-week dinner party to introduce me and two others to her guest of honour, a woman the wrong side of 40 who has achieved much in her career. Nigella Express was duly consulted and great effort went into the dinner. Guest of Honour arrived on time, but the rest of us were late (mid-week dinner parties? In deepest Berkshire? What do you expect?). As a result, GoH was several glasses of wine to the good before we arrived.

As we moved to the dining table TG appeared with her lovingly prepared lamb casserole, single vegetable (a tasty concoction of cabbage and bacon) and rice. It was at this point that GoH revealed that she was vegetarian. The blood drained from TG's face. Nigella and fridge were hastily consulted and a piece of salmon was magicked from goodness knows where and shoved into the microwave. Poor GoH put on a brave face and managed a forkful or two before pushing it to one side.

Fuelled only by rice and wine, GoH proved very entertaining, even fessing up to having taken a lover more than 15 years younger than her. She has been seeing him once a month for a year and a half now. Even in the face of another Nigella special (some pear effort with Roquefort) at this point we forgot about the food and demanded all manner of detail. We were duly obliged, but I shall spare your blushes.

Food and sex are a fine combination, though, and both vital to a happy life. But what about books? I recently made an honourable exception and read a novel while not on holiday – but then it was by my Newest Girlfriend, Jeanette Winterson. Reading *The Stone Gods* was to prepare for visiting NG in east London at her shop, a perfectly preserved bit of Georgian England opposite a flash new office block. NG has delegated the shop to the charming Harvey. Harvey chooses all the food on sale and runs a thriving business selling bespoke sandwiches to lawyers and bankers, while NG confines herself to writing books and (at the moment) a children's television series.

*The Stone Gods*, I noticed, was on sale in NG's shop alongside the chocolate and preserves. As the next customer arrived to collect his sandwich, I stopped him and asked if he had read it. No, he said. When I asked if lesbian robots were perhaps not his thing, he scrutinised the front cover rather more keenly.

The lesbian robot in the book could technically also be described as disabled, since she ends up with only a head.

She doesn't need food, although she does seem to manage sex. Sexually active disabled lesbian robots make for more challenging reading than Nigella Express, though I'm afraid both are a little more than I can manage mid-week. I have told NG that I am going to return to *The Economist*, at least until the next Moneypenny family holiday, and will engage Harvey to cook my next dinner party.

## THE SECRET OF LONGEVITY
*Apr 5, 2008*

"England and America are two countries separated by a common language." If George Bernard Shaw were alive today, he might add that they are also separated by, among other things, 3,000 miles or so of sea and a totally different approach to advertisements for erectile dysfunction.

We might be separated by a common language but we are united in our fascination with the Eliot Spitzer saga; it got acres of news coverage in the British press, including the *FT,* as well as in the US. Who could resist the chance to read about the extra-curricular habits of a man who had set himself up as the scourge of Wall Street, and in so doing probably increased the sales of Starbucks in London several hundredfold by forcing analysts and investment bankers to go out for coffee if they wanted to speak to each other? In his blog, my *FT* colleague John Gapper produced a very early account of what was happening that proved to be gripping reading for two reasons. First, he swiftly received a post on the blog from a woman working as a highly paid escort in NYC (always interesting to see who reads the *FT* online), and second, that he included a link to scans of the court papers, which I read with great interest.

I was intrigued by one thing in particular, which was mentioned in both the court papers and the blog posting from the call girl – the length of time that escorts are booked for. No wonder Gapper's correspondent says that she spends most of her time with her clothes on – when was the last time anyone you know had sex for four hours, the length of a typical Emperors Club booking? Indeed, would you want to have sex for four hours? The very thought of it makes me feel exhausted. Does one get a break for a drink and a visit to the loo, I wonder? I considered the four-hour question on my way over the pond last week for a few days stateside, particularly as I read several magazines during the flight. Many British commentators followed Gapper's lead and addressed the issue of sex for money, including Taki Theodoracopulos in *The Spectator*. Taki was delighted at Spitzer's demise, not least because Spitzer was responsible for instigating the prosecution of Taki's friend, Hank Greenberg, former chairman of AIG, a big US insurer. Greenberg, for the record, has denied all the charges brought against him and has not been convicted of wrongdoing. Even those of us who are not Greek millionaires and don't hang out with insurance billionaires can admire Greenberg's achievements (and they are many – he served in the Second World War and the Korean War with distinction, and then took charge of an ailing AIG in the 1960s and led it back to health with resounding success).

Taki's views on Spitzer closely resemble his views on Hillary Clinton, but on reading yet another of his rather subjective swipes at her I realised I was just as guilty of trite comments with little foundation. Taki suggested last month that Clinton should not win the Democratic nomination because he did not find her attractive enough. Does that amount to trivialising the debate? No more so, perhaps, than my assertion earlier this year that I would vote for Clinton (if I could) because she is a woman. I realise, having had it pointed out to me that I am always the first to resist any form of positive discrimination, that even if I were privileged enough to have a say in the process, I ought to base my voting decision on the candidate's record rather than her sex.

Once in the US and ensconced in a hotel room, I immersed myself in wall-to-wall CNN to hear how the race for the Democratic nomination was going. It was then that I suddenly realised why people in the US book escorts for such long periods of time. Listening to yet another television advertisement for erectile dysfunction while brushing my teeth, I caught the disclaimer for the first time.

We in Britain have lengthy disclaimers at the end of TV advertisements too, you know, although they are more along the lines of "you could lose your home if you do not keep up repayments" (judging by what is happening in the US, this is a line the Americans don't include in theirs very often). But the disclaimer that I was suddenly drawn to was rather different. It suggested that if the drug being advertised was still working after four hours you should call the doctor. Four hours? Now I understand

## HEIGHTS OF POWER
*Apr 12, 2008*

Warm and comfortable. No, that's not a description of my personality and figure, but the dress code on the invitation for my recent ladies' shooting day. Every year I ask a select group of women with whom I do business to join me in a day's clay

pigeon shooting. We start with breakfast, have some tuition/
practice, break for elevenses and then hold a competition before
lunch. Carriages, as they say on the poshest invitations, are at
2.30pm.

I was pretty pleased with myself for assembling a group of
women who, more than ever before, were at the top of their
profession or business. Many of them had not shot before - but
that was the whole point. The more people I can get to enjoy
my leisure interests, the more I will get to pursue them. The
more businesswomen I can encourage to enjoy shooting, goes
the logic, the more companions I will have with whom to share
my favourite pursuit. I just need to show them how relaxing it
is. I have found that there is nothing (aside from prescription
drugs) better able to erase all else from my mind than tracking a
clay across the sky and trying to shatter it into tiny pieces. And
when that happens, the satisfaction of having hit something is
(almost) better than sex.

On the morning of my ladies' day last year, I arrived back
from the US. As I came down the steps of the plane at Luton the
rain was going sideways and it even started to hail at one point.
Chastened by the experience, this year I encouraged everyone to
wrap up warm. And they took me at my word – many came in
woolly hats, almost all wore Wellington boots and several didn't
even bother with make-up, which is quite remarkable when you
consider that most of us were over 40. I even had lunch with my
Wellington boots on – not unremarkable for the shooting field
but not your usual luncheon attire anywhere else.

No dress code was attached to the invitation I received to
lunch with the first lady of France – an event that took place
on my 46th birthday. Madame Sarkozy, or Carla Bruni as she
is occasionally called, was being hosted by our own first lady,
Sarah Brown, at Lancaster House. One hundred and twenty
women from the media, business and art worlds were there,
and for a few of us it was a reunion from my shoot a week or
two before. In spite of the lack of a dress code, I suspected that
Wellington boots were not the order of the day this time, so I
went out and bought some proper shoes.

Unlike many women I know, I am not obsessed with shoes.
But I did think that, for a lunch hosted by the wife of the
Labour Prime Minister for the First Lady of France, I might
buy some French shoes with red soles. Thus I found myself
looking at Christian Louboutin's creations. I only looked at
them, as it turned out, not because of the cost (they aren't all
£400-plus. I am sure the more budget-conscious of you will
be relieved to discover that there are some on Net A Porter for
less than £300!), but for a more practical reason. Have you ever
contemplated walking around on 140mm heels? It would give
me vertigo.

So I bought some Louboutin lookalikes in black patent (and
without red soles) that had heels a mere 100mm high, though
even these were bad enough. Why I did this, I have no idea.
I had to totter past assorted paparazzi in absurdly impractical
shoes and then up two flights of stairs in Lancaster House
– and all for what? You can imagine that, while women are
notoriously critical of each other's dress sense, no one would
be looking at me if Carla Bruni was on display. Indeed, not
only Carla Bruni. On my table alone I had Kelly Hoppen, the
glamorous interior designer, and Kathy Lette (oh, for the figure
to be able to wear a mini-skirt in the year I turn 50).

I nearly fell over twice on my way back down the stairs at
Lancaster House, and then staggered out past the paparazzi
and fell into a cab. The shoes, a snip at £100, will probably be
consigned to the mantelpiece. They were neither warm, nor
comfortable. My Wellington boots, which cost £200, would
have been both. And they are French. Next time, Carla!

## FISCAL JERKS
*Apr 19, 2008*

Do you prefer your taxes arising or on remittance? I suspect
that, like most of us, you would rather pay no tax at all. But
if you are one of the 114,000 people living in the UK and
registered as non-domiciled then you will have a vested interest
in the difference between these two ways of assessing your
taxable income.

If you wish to continue to be taxed on remittance – ie to pay tax only on income earned in the UK and that remitted to Britain, leaving all your offshore income and capital gains undeclared to Her Majesty's Revenue & Customs – then you will now have to pay a £30,000 ($59,120) annual surcharge. Plus you lose your personal tax allowance. So unless you are Roman Abramovich you are going to feel substantially lighter in the purse.

In 1776, the economist Adam Smith said that a good tax system had four qualities. It should be equitable, certain, convenient and efficient. In my view the domicile rule does not – before or after the changes – pass these tests.

I am not at all sure that the ability of some UK residents to avoid paying tax on offshore income and capital gains is equitable; the way tax policy in the UK seems to change on a whim makes our system anything but certain; I don't find my tax return particularly convenient to fill in; and as for efficiency, every government department has room for improvement.

The screams from certain quarters about the unfairness of the new tax can be heard all the way across the Atlantic. Depending on whom you listen to, these 114,000 "non-doms" are key to the UK's arts organisations/charities/financial services industry and if you tax them in this way they will all leave and the world will come to an end. This, the argument goes, is because they are the only people who can afford to support anything, and because we would lose some of the best financial brains in the world if we don't give them preferential tax status.

Really? On the money side of things, non-domiciled millionaires live in the UK precisely because they don't want to pay tax here. So they don't bring their money, in which case there's no benefit to the UK in having them. And on the idea that the City of London would lose its most talented people if all the non-doms left? If we are dependent for our global pre-eminence as a financial centre on foreigners then we are in a sorry state.

Like every democratic nation, we have a means to change unpopular tax policies: vote against them. Most of the 114,000 non-doms will have a vote (we are even more generous with our votes over here than we are with our taxation; even Mr M, an Australian through and through, has a vote). It is unlikely, however, that the non-doms will be able to use their votes to much effect. First, because there are not many of them. Second, because both the government and the opposition have said that they intend to tax non-doms. And finally, because we are at least a year away from a general election.

We are of course much closer to London's Mayoral election on May 1. Boris Johnson has shortened his odds of success but before voting for him – or indeed anyone else – I want to know what their position is on non-doms, or rather one non-domicile in particular. It is said that Boris supports the campaign to have a statue of Sir Keith Park, a New Zealander and hero of the first and second world wars, placed on the fourth plinth in Trafalgar Square. But does he? Boris, we want to know where you stand on where Sir Keith should stand!

No, the real problem non-doms have in the UK is not how they are taxed, but how they are regarded. The press has had a field day with the 114,000. My Non-Domiciled Girlfriend sums it up when she says that she now feels like a target of generic ill-will, a victim of the fiscal equivalent of ethnic cleansing.

I have maintained for a long time that the greatest threat the UK faces in hanging on to our high achievers – to their talent and their money – is the actions of the media. Britain can seem a hostile place if the press decides it doesn't like you. Regardless of how you pay your taxes.

## THE BEST-LAID CHILDCARE PLANS OF MOTHERS AND MEN
*Apr 26, 2008*

So what do you think of our new livery? In the magazine world redesigns do not happen casually. They require careful planning, attention to detail, hard work by lots of people and, finally, delivery of the longed-for event.

And it's not just magazine redesigns that need all this. So as I went away recently on a two-week business trip, I spent days explaining to everyone that while I was absent, Cost Centres

#2 and #3 had to be sent off to camps (yes, different ones, and in different parts of the country) for a week. Lists were made of clothes and kit required. CC#2, going to Devon, had to be deposited at a motorway service station to meet a coach coming from London. CC#3 then had to be driven to his camp in Dorset. Between the nanny, my mother, Mr M and the CCs themselves, surely this was possible.

I was in Dubai on business, but in June Mr M is going there to meet his mother for a couple of days and play golf with a reader of this column. This gentleman made the mistake of copying me in on an e-mail he had sent to the *FT* on the subject of golf, and, noticing his location, I wrote and asked if he would host Mr M for a round while he was in Dubai. To my delight, he agreed. So now Mr M is going to play golf with a total stranger in June. I thought I should check him out on my visit just in case he turned out to be an axe murderer.

Not a bit of it. He is Australian, grew up in Melbourne, has worked at the same bank for 28 years and has Mr M's approach to the whole sport-life balance. He and his wife kindly invited me to dinner and so I sat watching the sun set over the Arabian Gulf with a glass of champagne in my hand. My host confessed to a golf handicap of five, and an in-depth knowledge of golf websites. He also had houseguests, he told me, a New Zealand couple. Five minutes later Jeff Crowe appeared and promptly got busy with the barbecue.

Former New Zealand Test cricketers cooking dinner at the house of an Australian who plays golf off five? The wrong Moneypenny was at this dinner party. I called Mr M (interrupting the packing) so that he could participate at a distance. "Jeff Crowe's there?" said Mr M, before rattling off Crowe's career statistics and then reminding me that he had played against Crowe at some schoolboy tournament in 1975. 1975? I handed the phone over.

The two of them discussed that tournament as if it were yesterday.

The day of the departure for the CCs' camp arrived. So, in the UK, did several inches of snow. The nanny had done the packing and, in what she no doubt regarded as a sweet touch for two brothers about to be parted for a week, gave them matching cases.

Mr M drove the 4WD through deep snow to the service station, handed over CC#2, and set off for deepest Dorset. On arrival he went to get CC#3's coat out of his case... and realised that he had the wrong one. By the time he had driven across to north Devon and back to Dorset and then back to Oxfordshire, all CCs had the right clothes and he had spent seven hours on the road during the worst day for driving so far this year. He called when he got home.

It was early the next day for me and I was on the next leg of my trip, watching the sun rise across the Tasman Sea. I tried to sound sympathetic. But the truth is that there is no substitute for careful planning, attention to detail and hard work by lots of people if you want to ensure successful delivery. What do you think?

## THE DOMINO THEORY OF TEENAGE NUTRITION
*May 10, 2008*

Pizza parenting. That's the social phenomenon that I believe explains Domino's recent results. In the statement issued at the annual general meeting on April 24, Stephen Hemsley, executive chairman of Domino's, which is about to move from Aim to the main list, said: "I am pleased to report a strong start to the year." He went on to say that in the 16 weeks to April 20 2008 like-for-like sales in the group's 450 "mature" outlets were up 13.3 per cent. I am not surprised.

Are you a pizza parent? Try out this question at the next dinner party you attend. Cost Centre #1, now 18 and about to sit his A-levels, called up from school last Sunday evening. He had been out late on Saturday (socialising) and spent much of the next day sitting mock examinations. He had then unintentionally missed dinner, which on Sunday is at an earlier time. He was hungry, and had no money for food.

As you can imagine, I had very forthright views on this. If he had spent his money unwisely the night before, and then been sufficiently disorganised to miss school dinner, he should go hungry. The important thing about mistakes is to learn from them. How would he learn to be better with money, and more organised, if we always bailed him out? I told him I was aware that he was hungry, but I was miles away. What did he expect me to do about it? I put down the telephone.

After a few minutes, a text message arrived. "Dear Mum," it read. "The number of Domino's Pizza in Crowthorne is ... I'd like a 'Meateor' pizza please, delivered to the Porter's Lodge. It should be £9.99 on the college deal. Cheers, Mum, give them my number."

I walked straight down the hall and handed the phone to his father. Mr M was, unsurprisingly, watching golf. What did he think I should do? Should I buy the pizza?

Parenting is a tough business and is undertaken by millions of people each year with no relevant qualifications. I have never had an 18-year-old son before, let alone a hungry one away at boarding school. My initial reaction was to text him back and tell him to starve. At moments like this, I often suspect I am the worst parent in the world.

It was maybe with that in mind that my Longest Standing Girlfriend, and another Former Schoolfriend, planned a reunion evening with me. FS is one of those enviable women who have married well (currently FS's husband is finance director of the most famous insurance institution in the world) and despite having devoted herself to the care and upbringing of her children, still looks fresh and slim and elegant. LSG, too, has prioritised her children and only worked part-time since they arrived.

The two of them took me to the theatre to see *God of Carnage*. If you think you are a dysfunctional parent (or even that you are in a dysfunctional marriage), go and see this. It will cheer you up – either because it will make you laugh, or because you will benchmark yourself against the characters and feel better about yourself. Either way, this play, about two sets of parents who meet up to discuss a playground incident in which one child has hit another with a stick (90 minutes, without an interval) stars four very accomplished actors: Ralph Fiennes, Ken Stott, Janet McTeer and Tamsin Greig. Tamsin who? She plays Debbie in *The Archers*, and in real life has three children, but if I ever meet her, my most pressing question will not be whether she thinks Brian should divide the farm between his children, or even if she would, in real life, organise a pizza delivery to her child's school. It would be how she manages to vomit so convincingly on stage.

I did order the pizza, by the way. It was weak of me, I know, and I am sure that none of you would have. But it wasn't out of pity for my son, incarcerated at boarding school from the age of seven. It was because I knew that if I didn't, I wouldn't get a wink of sleep, and I had a crucial meeting the next day. Mr Hemsley, be grateful for pizza parents.

## AT LAST, I'M BACK IN THE RING
*May 17, 2008*
Four months have sped by. In early January I had some surgery and as a result had to give up aerobic exercise – ie, boxing – for many weeks. For someone who had paid only lip service to regular exercise before 2003, I was surprisingly disturbed by having to stay away from the gym. Asked by a friend, back in 2002, why I didn't exercise, I replied (truthfully) that my size and shape didn't worry me. They have never stood in the way of personal and professional goals – if I wanted the kind of job or man who was looking for Claudia Schiffer then maybe I might have done something about it. But what about my husband and children, my friend asked. Even if I didn't exercise for fitness then surely I would like to stay alive long enough to look after them?

Four months later and I am back in the boxing ring. And not just in any boxing ring – the weekend I returned to aerobic exercise saw the arrival in Southampton of the Independence of the Seas, the largest cruise ship in the world.

It's a shared title as she has two equally large sisters – but she will be the only one of the three to be based (home-ported, as they say in the trade, sounds rather like something out of

*Doctor Who*) in Europe. All of them have full-size boxing rings in their gyms, plus heavy bags and other pugilistic equipment. Invited for the onboard celebrations of her Southampton debut straight from the builder's yard (and what a yard that must be – she is 160,000 tonnes and 1,112ft long), I looked at the schedule of entertainment in search of a suitable time-slot to slip away to the gym. In common with other cruise lines, Royal Caribbean (the Independence's owner) has strong links with the community in Southampton, so I was not surprised that the girl scouts had been invited to sing during the afternoon. I decided that this would be the event I would miss.

Wraps already on, I arrived in a near-deserted gym. Fifteen minutes later, Cost Centre #2 came rushing in, dripping wet from the pool. "Mum, Mum, where's the camera?" He's 13 now, so girls are becoming more important and I assumed that Southampton must boast some very attractive girl scouts. Then Mr M came in (so much for a peaceful time in the gym) saying that the pop music was too loud for him. Pop music? It turned out that it was not the local girl scouts entertaining the guests around the pool, it was a band called Scouting for Girls – who are, as it happens, all boys. I had never heard of them but CC#2 thought they were a very big deal and we now have a range of photographs of him with various band members.

It is not just Royal Caribbean that has taken delivery of a new boxing ring. A week after my girl-scout experience I was at another day of celebrations: the official opening of South Moreton Boxing Club's extension, together with a second boxing ring. This didn't boast a chart-topping band, but the day did start with the blessing of both rings by the newly installed local vicar.

I confess that while "off games", as it were, I resorted to Pilates. This was not only to keep me in the habit of attending exercise (if you can call it that) regularly, but also so that I could catch up most weeks with my Pilates-Loving Girlfriend, who is even busier than me. So, my flexibility has increased and my posture is better – but I weigh 3kg more than I did at Christmas. That means I also need to get back in training with

Holly the Sadist at the Royal Automobile Club. There's no boxing ring there, but HTS and I regularly don the wraps and gloves to make sure the work-out doesn't grow too tedious. I've also gone back to my local (now two-ring) gym for Saturday-morning circuit training. It's women only and costs £10 – come and join me. As I worked up a sweat I thought about how it was keeping me fit and well so that the three CCs and Mr M need never worry about where their next clean pair of socks or hot meal is coming from. On reflection, if that is why I am doing this, maybe another four months off won't hurt.

## WHY I NEED TO BE A PARTY INSIDER
*May 24, 2008*

I never want a surprise party. I like parties – I like giving them, I like going to them. But a surprise party? For me? No, thank you.

Last weekend I attended a surprise 49th birthday party thrown for my Most Telegenic Girlfriend. She is a former TV newsreader and reporter, and her loving boyfriend decided that a surprise party was a great idea. He co-opted one of her best friends – my Most Glamorous Girlfriend – to arrange it all. His only contribution, aside from having the idea, was to make sure that MTG was kept out of the way all day and delivered back to her house at 7.30pm, dressed to kill.

That's one of the reasons I would hate a surprise party – if you don't know about it, how can you be sure you're wearing the right thing? MTG's boyfriend went to meet her at the beauty therapist, where he had made sure she spent the afternoon, and took her some clothes that he had picked from her wardrobe. I doubt that Mr M could name one item in my wardrobe, let alone be trusted to pick something for me to wear to a party.

And who would he invite to my party? Would he leave out all those friends of mine who he doesn't like, or the ones whose husbands he doesn't like, or all the men he suspects I secretly (or not so secretly) fancy? (In which case it might be quite a subdued gathering.) And where would he hold it – the golf club?

This surprise party was at MTG's house. Given she shares it with her three children, all of school age, it is not surprising that when MGG arrived to let the caterers in, she decided to put a vacuum cleaner over the floor. Actually, that's a lie – MGG doesn't do vacuum cleaners. She got her son (age nine) to do it. Then my Journalist Girlfriend turned up. JG is one of those women who, irritatingly, looks 10 years younger than she is, and attributes this to constant moisturising. In fact, she lists moisturising on her CV under interests, and uses up to eight different ones each day. You would think with all this moisturising she wouldn't have time to go to work, let alone attend surprise parties, but somehow she manages. On arrival, she inspected the bathroom (no ground-floor loo in MTG's house, so guests would have to use the first-floor bathroom). She then called MGG up to help her fix it up.

A family bathroom used daily by three children is bound to need a little sprucing up. However, I cannot think of two less likely people to give it up-close-and-personal attention than MGG and JG. They are both incredibly house-proud, but as I said, MGG doesn't really do housework, (that's what staff are for) and I doubt that JG would risk her hands without pre- and post-housework moisturising. Apparently they went round the whole room (including the loo!) with a brush, a cloth and bleach.

Of course, there were other blips: no one could find MTG's cutlery canteen, they covered the tables with duvet covers to start with before finding the tablecloths, and they had to reorganise MTG's fridge to get everything in.

MTG's boyfriend brought her home where she was confronted by caterers in her kitchen, a fork shortage and her linen cupboard devoid of duvet covers and white tablecloths. Not to mention an immaculately clean toilet and bathroom, and about 30 people in her garden. Amazingly, she took this all in her stride, and even appeared moved to tears as we all shouted "happy birthday".

It was a lovely party. The food was delicious, the house and garden looked pristine, the guests were warm and friendly

and the birthday girl looked beautiful and not a day over 40.
How thoughtful, everyone said, of her boyfriend to arrange
it. No! No! If Mr M is reading this, I never want him to invite
random girlfriends into my house (however much I like them),
to vacuum my floor, rifle through my fridge and linen cupboard
and – worst of all – clean my loo. If he ever does that, there
definitely would be tears. Please, no surprise parties for me.

## FOREVER SIPPING BUBBLES
*May 31, 2008*
In 2002 I embarked on a love affair that has continued ever
since. No, not with a man (or a woman!) but with a champagne.
On a summer's evening that year someone handed me a glass
of champagne. As I drank it, I could taste why it cost so much.
From that moment, I was hooked.

I only happened to drink that champagne because I was a
contributor to *FT Weekend*, and so it was entirely appropriate
that when I recently embarked on a 24-hour champagne tasting,
I should have started at an *FT Weekend* party. This had all
the hallmarks of class that you would expect of a publication
such as this one (including an elegant and never-before used
Christopher Wren interior, complete with a Henry Moore
sculpture) and, of course, copious quantities of champagne.
And not just any champagne – Bollinger's recently released La
Grande Année Rosée 1999, which is the same colour as the *FT's*
paper.

Notwithstanding my main champagne love affair, I am partial
to the odd glass of pink. It is made by blending a little red wine
with champagne and is totally unrelated to the glasses of pink
bubbly that I am occasionally handed on game shoots, which
are made up of sloe gin (a shooting staple) and champagne.
This is apparently known as a "slogasm" but is to be avoided
not only for its awful name but also because it is ruinous to my
shooting. The Bollinger, by contrast, was very pleasant and
entirely fitting for the occasion.

And so, when I continued my 24-hour tasting the following
morning, at England's first Test match against New Zealand, it

had set a high standard.

Being in a box at Lord's on a day when the first few hours of play are rained off is a networking opportunity par excellence, and champagne helps. I was being entertained in the Mound Stand, which is in a prime position to watch play, and also a prime position (as the Mound Stand curves – well designed, Sir Michael Hopkins) to see who is in all the other boxes. As the rain continued I was able to spot key people, go and knock on the door of the box, champagne (MCC's Gardet) in hand, to show that I was a guest in another box – and say: "I see so and so is in here and just wanted to say 'hello'." If you were at the first day's play and saw a random, slightly overweight middle-aged woman march into your box and embrace a man over 50, that was me.

Being married to an MCC playing member, I know that the MCC champagne sells for less per six-bottle case than a single bottle of my much-loved favourite, so in search of a slightly better drinking experience I moved on, during a break in the afternoon's play, to the Grand Stand. This was designed by Sir Nicholas Grimshaw, who clearly didn't understand the need to network at cricket matches (it doesn't curve at all). Thus, from the ECB box I could only peer into the two boxes immediately adjacent (BSkyB and the MCC box itself) to see if there was anyone I should be saying hello to.

The Deutsche Bank box was also nearby, but as I was not born with a giraffe-like neck I could not manage to lean out and see if Anshu Jain was sitting in it – an even more important fact to ascertain before storming it than if it merely served quality champagne.

The ECB has a relatively new chairman which might or might not account for the excellent quality both of guests and of champagne. On the guest front, I spent some time chatting to Bill Emmott, my favourite ex-editor of *The Economist*, who has just published Rivals: How the Power Struggle Between China, India and Japan Will Shape Our Next Decade.

This is a better name for a book than slogasm is for a drink, but, even so, it could perhaps have been a little catchier, shall we say. Notwithstanding its name, the book is a good read and we discussed it while sipping Veuve Clicquot, a champagne that I have remained almost entirely faithful to since drinking it as an undergraduate. Until, that is, I fell in love.

## WHERE NETWORKING BLOSSOMS
*Jun 07, 2008*

Gardens were not on the agenda. The purpose of the Chelsea Flower Show Gala Preview is not, as I have explained before, to preview any flowers. It represents the largest annual gathering of corporate Britain, the whole exercise paid for in large part by banks and other professional advisers (credit crunch? What credit crunch?) That the Chelsea Preview is such a hot ticket is largely explained by the attraction it holds for the executive spouses - still largely female - who get to view the gardens, floral displays and other horticulture-related items in a crowd of around 5,000. This might sound busy, but it is positively sparse when you consider that about 700,000 people would pass through the Royal Hospital Road site during the next five days.

My executive (Australian) spouse does not do the Flower Show. That day he was playing golf at Royal Birkdale, on the 2008 Open Championship course, in the *Financial Times* Anglo Irish Bank Business Championship. His team members included MP and golfing writer Tim Yeo, National Farmers' Union director-general Richard Macdonald and stockbroker Nigel Marsh. The Mr M/Macdonald duo came in with a score of 42 and the Yeo/Marsh combo delivered 39, so on a total score of 81 they were leading for a while and busy working out how they could adjust their October schedules to make it to the finals in Portugal. Sadly for them, Wilson Decorators pipped them to the post with 84; but Nigel Marsh, the youngest member of the Moneypenny team, claimed the nearest-the-pin honours and was presented with an Odyssey White Hot putter. What is a White Hot putter? Sounds like something you might find in the obscure garden implements section of the Chelsea Flower Show.

The hottest thing at this year's show was not a garden, but a gardener. My Divorced Girlfriend found me pausing to draw breath between CEOs and insisted that I accompany her to see the Australian garden. As her company was sponsoring a (different) garden she had been there all afternoon showing it to the Queen, the press and sundry others. She had therefore also had a chance to spot other highlights of the flower show. I explained that I wasn't really there to see the gardens. No, she explained, it was not the garden that she wanted me to inspect but the garden designer.

Just to shut her up I followed DG to this garden, where two men were waiting to receive visitors. I marched up to them and started to explain that I was there because my friend wanted me to meet the handsomest man at the show, and please could they tell me which of them it was so that I could shake his hand and then get on with my networking. I got about halfway through that before I looked into the eyes of Jamie Durie and realised why I was there.

Now, as I explained to him, I had never heard of Jamie Durie. I am not interested in gardening and although I visit Australia and the US reasonably regularly I have no idea who is presenting TV gardening shows in these countries. I have also never watched the Oprah Winfrey show, where Jamie appeared to some acclaim. We have a version of Jamie Durie in the UK, Alan Titchmarsh - though I can't imagine my 40-something girlfriends salivating over him in the way DG was over Jamie. Neither can I imagine Alan Titchmarsh ever working as a male stripper, as Jamie did in his youth. He led the Manpower revue, an Australian version of the Chippendales, before setting up his garden design company in 1996. He is serious eye candy, and also very entertaining to talk to, if a bit young for me (he was 38 last Tuesday). Plus, as HRH the Duke of Edinburgh discovered, he knows a thing or two about plants.

Jamie's fellow garden host at the time I met him was Julian Brady, the General Manager of his company, PATIO. Julian, if you are reading this, you are not bad-looking either, but you need to update the awards on your website. Jamie's garden won a gold medal at Chelsea. (Question for the Royal Horticultural

Society: how many of your judges are female and have a
pulse?) Mr M is determined not to be a medal-free Australian.
He is going to have another go at winning, this time at the
Royal Liverpool on July 9, when I shall be at a charity shoot.
Golf, I am afraid, is never on my agenda.

### BENIGN NEGLECT OF CARS AND COST CENTRES
*Jun 14, 2008*

An extra night in his own bed. That was the prize won by CC#3
for breaking his arm. He had gone to play with a friend in
the village whose mother called, saying he had slipped while
playing in the garden and fallen badly. It was an hour before
he was due to return to school at the end of a long weekend.
How badly had he hurt himself, I inquired. "I think it could be
serious," she said. "He's asking for his mother."

My children are famously self-sufficient. When I was asked
once by the BBC what I attributed this to I answered in one
word - neglect. So when one of them wants his mother it is
usually a Major Incident. I hurried round to the friend's house
and brought home a rather pale nine-year-old. His arm appeared
to be in one piece, he could still squeeze my hand when I asked,
and the sister in charge of the sick bay at school is a fully
qualified medical professional, so I sent him back to school.

The school was having none of it. Mr M, who was on
chauffeur duty, was sent off to Newbury Accident &
Emergency. Here (as you would expect on a bank holiday
Monday night) he waited patiently for an hour for CC#3 to
be seen, and then another hour or so for him to be X-rayed.
Father and son took this in good spirits and were infinitely more
understanding of the delay than I would have been, so the right
parent was definitely on hand. By the time they had diagnosed a
fracture in the greater tubercle of his humerus that could not be
set, had issued a sling and some painkillers and sent CC#3 on
his way, it was much too late for him to return to school.

I promise I was on stand-by to drop everything and rush
down there if they had decided to set it, and I made him a hot
water bottle when he came home. But I felt so guilty about not

being more sympathetic that a couple of weeks later I got up very early on a Sunday morning and took him to participate in a children's penalty shoot-out competition at Chelsea FC's ground at Stamford Bridge. He did very well, even with his arm in a sling.

The competition preceded a charity football tournament into which I had entered an office team, comprising our two football-playing members of staff and several business associates. We started in spectacular style, beating a team from *The Telegraph* 3-0, but it all went downhill from there. I was determined to stay until the team's last match, whatever their performance, but CC#3 was losing his enthusiasm. My Pilates-Loving Girlfriend was there and suggested that he go home with her children and have tea. I could collect him later.

I did hesitate - PLG's house is in the opposite direction to the school and he had to be back at 7pm if the school's Sunday evening routine was to be observed. But he was keen to go and so I said yes, after calculating that I would have enough time to collect him and make it back to Newbury.

But I had reckoned without one important point. PLG lives in what one could describe as a gated community, with serious security. Despite having visited her several times over the years, I have never driven there in my own car. Before I could drive up to PLG's house the car had to be searched.

I was asked, not unreasonably, to open the bonnet of the car. I have had the car for two years, but in all that time I have never had to do this. I guessed, correctly, that there must be a button to release the catch, but could I find it? Eventually I got the handbook out of the glove box and the policeman and I studied it carefully. Had I never had to top up the washer fluid, he asked. "Don't be silly," I said. "What do you think husbands are for?"

It was a full 30 minutes from arriving at the gate to presenting myself at PLG's front door. Driving back, I had to call the school and explain that my incompetence as a car mechanic matched my incompetence as a parent, and that CC#3 would not be coming back to school on time. Yet another extra night in his own bed.

## LESSONS FOR LIFE OVER A TRICKY CUP OF INSTANT
*July 05, 2008*

First impressions count. At our office we are careful to make
sure that every visitor is made to feel extremely welcome: they
are greeted at the door, shown to a meeting room and offered
tea, coffee or a cold drink. The person meeting them will be
smartly dressed. He or she will smile and offer to take their coat
or bag, will show them to the bathroom if required and will
generally make them feel special. Even our coffee is special,
since my team have long insisted on having those plunger-type
filter coffee pots (which I have never worked out how to use),
so that they can make it fresh each time.

But even the best-laid plans can sometimes go awry. One
day last week the electricity provider for central London
discovered a fault and told us at 6pm that we were going to be
without power for the rest of the evening while it was repaired.
Although I was staying in the office that night (yes, I have a
bedroom in the office, how sad is that?), I was going to be out
all evening reviewing the papers for the BBC, accompanied
by our office manager who was going to stay in the spare
room (even sadder). I have to be accompanied by someone
as the papers are always full of football stories, which I don't
understand at all. Once again, this proved a winning ploy as
Thierry Henry had scored an own goal to help send France out
of Euro 2008, and for some reason this event had made all the
newspapers. Why?

We returned to the office at midnight and found our way
upstairs to bed by torchlight. However, the office's emergency
lights had all come on in the second bedroom where our office
manager was planning to sleep, and couldn't be switched off.
So we dragged a mattress to the floor below and she was finally
able to go to sleep – only to be woken at 3.30am when the
electricity came back on and all the printers sprang into life.

The power didn't stay on for long. At noon it disappeared
again, this time with no warning. After being told that there

was little chance of it being restored before midnight (leaving us without phones, a door bell and computer access), we decided to send everyone home who didn't have meetings that afternoon. This left a skeleton staff and our IT contractor.

Now, our IT contractor is very good at his job and has looked after us for years, but he has one major disadvantage. He doesn't speak English. I don't know what he does speak as I have never successfully identified it, but on being asked a question (e.g. Why am I suddenly getting spam again?) he replies at length in a language that I don't understand. I have learned to bypass these conversations directly and instead turn to others for translation services, including my office manager (on days when she has had a decent night's sleep).

So when our contractor came into a (darkened) meeting room later that afternoon, and explained that he had let someone in at the front door and what should he do with them, I realised that he had been, for that person, their first encounter with our company. Had he put them in a room? No. Had he offered them a drink? No. Had he even managed to communicate with them in English? I didn't dare ask.

A few days later, and with electricity miraculously restored, I had an early meeting arranged at the office. I was ready and waiting, opened the door myself and let the visitor in. I showed her to the meeting room and offered her a drink. She opted for coffee. I explained that as it was early, the Lovely Lucinda had not yet arrived, and so the coffee would be instant. The visitor looked slightly horrified and said that, in that case, she would prefer tea.

I convened an emergency meeting in the kitchen with the only other person in the office, the summer intern. As with most summer interns, she had a CV that puts mine to shame – a string of A*s at GCSE, straight As at A-level and on course for an impressive degree at Bristol. Plus a list of achievements that showed her to be impossibly musically talented. However, there was nothing to indicate that she might be able to operate a coffee plunger. I explained the problem to her. "Leave it to me," she said. "I was a waitress in my gap year." This last, of course, was not on her CV. First impressions may not be accurate.

## A NIGHT ON THE (BATHROOM) TILES
*July 12, 2008*
Clean and well-stocked bathrooms are critical. That's what I
told the cleaner last week before the Mother-in-Law arrived
for one of her State Visits. MIL lives in Sydney, which is far
enough away from the Moneypenny homestead to mean that
I encounter her at most once a year. That, by the way, is not
deliberate: I am blessed with a vigorous and clever mother-in-
law who is good company and very caring. But she does adore
one person – her only son – above all others, and I suspect she
wonders whether he married someone who looks after him quite
well enough.

MIL has not been on a state visit to England for more than 10
years. Her arrival this time coincided with my Ducal Girlfriend
hosting a cricket match in which Mr M was invited to play.
What better way to see England, I thought, than to stay with a
Duchess in a proper castle? So I persuaded DG to include MIL.
The cricket match launched the Belvoir Castle Cricket Trust,
which will preserve the ground and make it available during the
week to many deserving causes. I missed the match as I was
working but joined them in the evening for another of DG's
events, a Katherine Jenkins open-air concert.

Katherine Jenkins, like DG, is very beautiful, Welsh and can
sing. (DG trained as a singer and won many competitions in her
youth before giving it all up to marry a man with a large castle
and bear him five children.) I arrived very late to find that the
picnic dinner (lovingly packed into hampers by Mrs Horton,
the butler's wife) had all been eaten. All, that is, apart from the
food on DG's plate, which hadn't been touched because she
was too busy looking after her guests. I took her plate and went
off to find her so that I could ask her whether she minded me
eating her dinner. She was at the back of the enclosure on her
hands and knees, scraping food off plates and behaving like
any hostess – titled or otherwise – who has invited 40 people
to an open-air concert and provided them with a picnic but not
enough glassware, and has forgotten to pack bin liners. We

found a used wine glass, rinsed it out and then consumed a bottle of wine or so while singing along to Katherine Jenkins. Neither of us ended up eating much.

All 40 of us went back to DG's for a nightcap, including Ms Jenkins' supporting act, Blake. Blake is a foursome of young men who sing and wear dinner jackets, both to devastating effect. Someone had had the bright idea of setting up karaoke in DG's drawing room, and DG had the bright idea of inviting Blake to stay for the night. So it was that at around 1am you would have found DG's guests, butler and Blake singing along to "American Pie".

Fortunately MIL had gone to bed by then. I decided that I ought to as well, having moved on from the shared wine to champagne and then spirits. DG's castle has wonderfully well-stocked bathrooms with everything from bath oil to Tampax and hairdryers, so I went and had a long soak before climbing into the four-poster bed. Immediately I shut my eyes I realised that I had a problem. My head was spinning. Sensing that I might suddenly be rather ill, I took myself back to the bathroom. Here I felt better, but decided to position myself near the lavatory for a little while just in case. The sheepskin rug was comfy and the large fluffy white towels made for excellent emergency bedding. Mr M, having finished celebrating his unbroken last wicket partnership of 20 runs with Bill Frindall (he himself finished 18 not out), came to bed much later. He found the bed empty. Did he worry that I might have made off with one of Blake to a remote bedroom? I have no idea, but he did then decide to go to the loo and found his wife asleep on the floor. As he woke me up and put me to bed, he was muttering about the blasting he would have got in my column if it had been him on the bathroom floor. I wasn't listening. I was thinking how pleased I was going to be when I woke up that DG also keeps ibuprofen in her bathroom.

## RECLINE AND FALL
*July 19, 2008*
What do the governor of the Bank of England, the editor of this newspaper, the Mayor of London and I have in common?

Answer: we all sat in our seats on centre court until the very end of the thrilling Wimbledon men's final between Rafael Nadal and Roger Federer.

I have not had to sit so long in one place (and keep quiet) since Cost Centre #1 left school two weeks ago. Then we perched on the pews in the school chapel for an hour's service of thanksgiving (in particular we gave thanks that one child at least would no longer require school fees), followed by two stints of more than an hour each in which every one of about 200 children was given a citation by his housemaster or housemistress. That makes 199 children that did not belong to me whose citations I had to sit through. There was a break for a cup of tea in the middle, during which one impossibly slim mother remarked on how hard the pews were for those without ample padding of the posterior. I felt compelled to inform her that even those of us with plentiful padding in that department were finding it quite uncomfortable.

CC#1's house was called towards the end, by which time I was perfecting the art of sleeping while seated. Through a somnolent haze I heard his housemaster mention the words "modest", "humble", "scholar" and "achievement", and was then jolted awake by Mr M at which point I realised I had been listening to a description of Profit Centre #1, whose beaming parents were sitting across the aisle from us. (PC#1 is so called because I would pay good money to rent him from his parents and pass him off as my own. He has accompanied us on several family holidays over the years. On one such outing I had a screaming row with CC#1, about something trivial like bedtime or table manners. Turning in desperation to PC#1, I asked if he ever had arguments with his parents. "Oh yes", he said. About what? I asked. He thought about it a bit. "About whether or not I should do Greek GCSE." In another league, is PC#1.)

CC#2 starts at the school in September, so we have five years until we have to go through that experience again. I shall take a cushion next time. I wish the school luck with CC#2, he of the impossible questions. (Regular readers may remember "what is the point of opera if it doesn't make a profit" and "how many shares are there in issue of Vodafone".) This week's was "how do you calculate your Body Mass Index?". I pointed out that 1) I have no idea, 2) this is what is the internet is for and 3) even if I did know, I wouldn't be calculating mine. All I know is that in any medical check-up I have had recently, my BMI has been off the scale and into the section marked "imminent cardiac arrest". I must lose some weight.

Back at Wimbledon, Rafael Nadal finished the match lying on the floor. I was on the floor before it even started. Joining our host in a restaurant near Centre Court, a couple of hours before play began, I went to sit down. My host, who has impeccable manners, had stood up to greet me. He pulled the chair back and I sat down. On the floor. With the rain pouring down outside it did look for a moment as though the only entertainment the other diners could expect all afternoon was the sight of a middle-aged overweight mother of three struggling to get back on her feet without displaying too many of her undergarments. But we did get to see the match. Starting at about 2.30pm and interrupted twice by rain, it drew to a close after 9pm. Next year Centre Court will have a roof, so that should be the end of the problems with rain. It will also apparently have new (wider) seats. Not before time, especially if matches are going to take so long. Whoever put the seats in Centre Court was not expecting people with my BMI. And the other three people I mentioned at the start? Two were in the Royal Box (much wider seats) and one is blessed with a slender frame. Nothing in common with me, then.

## STUMPED BY THE BRITISH SUMMER
*July 26, 2008*

Summer has been here since April. No, I am not talking about the weather – if there has been any summer weather then I must have been asleep or in the bathroom (or both) when it happened, because all I can remember is rain and temperatures that have rarely risen above 19° C. My sleeveless shirts hang in the wardrobe unworn (at my age, bare arms probably aren't a good idea anyway), and the new garden furniture, procured especially for the state visit of the Mother-in-Law, remains unused.

The real reason that I know it is summer is that my three sons and husband are all playing cricket regularly. Ever since April, my weekends have been spent soaking rather nasty synthetic, cream-coloured trousers and very grubby socks and shirts in stain remover and then washing them at temperatures that I hope won't melt them. I used to long for old-fashioned cricket flannels but they would have to be ironed, so let's not go back to them.

For those of you who live in countries where cricket isn't played, I promise you that the hardest thing to get to grips with is not the rules – arcane and impenetrable though they are – but the appropriate laundry drill. The stains come in three varieties – mud, grass and the red that comes off cricket balls. Each requires a different strategy to dislodge it.

We were invited to play cricket as a family last weekend, although prior engagements meant that only the two younger Cost Centres and I could take part. Our hostess, my Investment Banker Girlfriend, has a magical home in the country which we all enjoyed visiting, and she laid on a lunch and tea that not even the most strenuous exercise could have offset. I did no exercise at all, not even the cricket, which was organised into five teams and played as a competition. The CCs were in the first game and so I stood at the boundary in suitable devoted-mother pose. IBG is the most considerate hostess and had risen at 6am to do the flowers personally – this in spite of her previous day's hard labour, hosting clients at Lord's for the England versus South Africa test match. Even with trips to Lord's and a CC of her own who is mad about cricket, I am not convinced that she has ever grasped much of the detail of the game. While I was watching, she came up and suggested that I come and sit down with a drink. I explained that I was needed on the boundary as the CCs were playing and indeed CC#2 was on strike. She suddenly looked very sympathetic. "Oh dear," she said, "why?"

If you don't understand that joke then you probably need a copy of a book called *Understanding Cricket*, which Mr M presented to me when we were married. It was an immaculate paperback and I asked him where he had bought it. He confessed that he had purchased it some years before – for his first wife. Perhaps its pristine condition offered a clue as to why the marriage did not last.

I should remind IBG that I took her to a breakfast recently to listen to Angela Knight, the CEO of the British Bankers' Association. Knight, who is a little older than IBG, explained that at school she and her fellow (female) pupils were taught to play cricket simply to ensure that they understood the rules and so would be less likely to make IBG-style howlers in later life. Perhaps we should reinstate this practice in all girls' schools. Back chez Moneypenny, we continue to play cricket come rain or shine. When we moved to this house we put up a county-standard cricket net on an artificial all-weather surface. We covered it in golf netting so that Mr M could tee off into it, too. After eight years here we shall be moving house this autumn, so by the time summer comes round again (or not, as the case may be), we shall have to build another one. Either that, or fix the weather in this part of the world.

## HOLIDAYS BEGIN AT THE AIRPORT
*August 09, 2008*

For my holiday this year I stayed at home. Yes, home. I don't mean that I went on holiday in England either. I mean that I just didn't go to work for two weeks.

You could make an economic case for this, but the truth is that I couldn't be bothered. If we go on a family holiday, who books it? Who makes sure everyone is packed? Who gets everyone up in time and then directs us to the correct long-term parking (which also has to be booked)? Who then spends the journey arbitrating between Cost Centres about who has whose iPod wireless headphones and other such disputes? And then, when we get there, who has to arrange the catering?

The phrase "self-catering holiday" is an oxymoron. For me, self-catering is never a holiday. It might be a holiday for everyone else, but who does the meal-planning and most of

the supermarket runs? Who does the laundry? Women might
have achieved equality in (some) careers and compensation, but
those of my generation certainly have not achieved it at home.
And definitely not on self-catering holidays.

It doesn't even work if you book a fully staffed villa – I did
that once, and arrived exhausted, only to find that I was still
expected to do all the menu planning. And, in my experience,
the alternative, a hotel, means suffering either hideous food or
heinous expense.
No, this year I stayed at home for two weeks and hired a cook.
I had done this before, several years ago, and have wonderful
memories of that summer, eating in the garden every day.
Sadly, I didn't manage to book the weather as well and so we
ate in the kitchen most days. But it did mean that I didn't see a
supermarket or peel a potato for the whole two weeks. Result!
And how did I occupy everyone? I sent Mr M to work (he has
had four overseas golf jaunts this year alone, so I thought that
was fair) and CC#1 was also working. So it was just the other
two, and I made sure that they had a steady supply of friends.
This gave me the opportunity to go flying every morning at
Oxford airport.

Yes, I am still learning to fly. Fixed wing, not rotary, for those
of you who are curious. I have not yet flown solo, but two
weeks of daily lessons have got me a lot closer. My vocabulary
is developing rapidly, for I am having to learn a whole new
language. For example, attitude is not something displayed by
teenage boys, and NSW is a meteorological term rather than a
state in Australia. It gave me great pleasure to add to the most
recent round of form-filling for keyman insurance that I was
learning to fly, which along with my body mass index must give
the underwriters something to get out their calculators for.

Like shooting, flying (at least at the beginning) allows no
room in your brain for anything other than remembering all the
things you are supposed to do to get up into the air and back
down again safely. Like taking your clothes off in front of a
new lover, much of learning to fly feels very strange at first, but
gets easier the more you do it. I welcome the utter concentration

required that stops me thinking about the unfairness of self-catering holidays, the cost of private education or indeed anything else. I also like learning again.

My instructor tells me that the three most useless things in aviation are 1) fuel in the bowser; 2) sky above you and 3) runway behind you. Oxford airport has a 1,553-metre runway that can take serious jets, so I can see it for miles around and never run out of room taking off or landing. Mr M is not a fan of me learning to fly, believing that it increases the odds of him being left to organise the self-catering holidays. But of course, if I ever qualify, I might be able to do everything one day. Book the villa, change the currency, fly the plane...

## THEIRS BUT TO DO OR DYE
*Aug 16, 2008*

There is more to life than hair, but it's a good place to start. For my female readers I am sure this rings true. Men have it so easy, don't they? Some of them might worry about being follically challenged, but maintaining what hair they do have is hardly taxing. We women have to worry about the cut, the colour, the style and, for those of us who appear in public from time to time, the need for a blow-dry. I am told by well-placed sources that the late Diana, Princess of Wales, saw the hairdresser every morning. So, I read, does Anna Wintour, editor-in-chief of American *Vogue*. Behind every woman of note, then, stands a hairdresser.

Consider the credit crunch. In Britain, the highest-profile casualty of this was Northern Rock, a bank that had relied on the wholesale money markets to fund its lending. When that supply of cash dried up, so did the bank. But at the point of crisis, when no one in the government could decide which of the Treasury, the Bank of England or the Financial Services Authority should be communicating with the media, who was the main beneficiary of this indecision? Answer: whoever is hairdresser to Angela Knight, the chief executive of the British Bankers' Association. Her constant appearances in broadcast and print media to comment on the Northern Rock debacle

47

plugged the gap left by our reticent regulators. Step forward, then, that man (or woman) whose livelihood received a direct boost from the collapse of the US subprime mortgage market.

I also make the occasional appearance on television, in my case once a month – an engagement for which I receive a (very) modest fee that is entirely accounted for by the taxman and the hairdresser. My hairdresser is Australian – selected not on the grounds of nationality but because he comes to the office to do my hair, which allows me to maximise my productivity. Have you noticed how many Australians choose not to live in Australia? It is not just my hairdresser and Mr M. List any number of world-famous Australians and you will find that most of them don't live in Australia. Clive James, Nicole Kidman, Kylie Minogue, Barry Humphries, Germaine Greer, Kathy Lette, James Wolfensohn, Greg Norman – they all live elsewhere, even if they have holiday homes in Australia. So many of them are not living there now that there is even an award for the Australian Businesswoman of the year in the UK. This was won on its inaugural presentation this year by my Information Technology Girlfriend, who no doubt went to the hairdresser before she collected it.

So I guess we should not be surprised that one of the world's bestselling hair treatments, the Aussie 3-Minute Miracle Reconstructor, is not made in Australia either (45 million bottles sold worldwide: you see, hair is crucial). The name and the kangaroo logo notwithstanding, this is a brand owned by Procter & Gamble, although it does contain Australian ingredients. So part of the £4.49 you part with in Boots is making its way Down Under.

This Australian/hairdressing connection continues. IT Girlfriend recently took me along to meet Julia Gillard and hear her speak. Who is Julia Gillard? She is deputy prime minister of Australia, the first woman in the post and, as such, is the highest-ranking woman in the history of the Australian government. Just to make sure she isn't lost for something to do all day, she is also the minister for education, the minister for employment and workplace relations and the minister for social inclusion. And who has this wonderwoman chosen as a boyfriend? His name is Tim Mathieson, and he is... a hairdresser.

## SLIGHTS OF HAND AND EYE
*Aug 23, 2008*

How do you handle rejection? I'm not good about it, on the whole. On the way to Los Angeles recently I noticed I was sitting close to a famous radio and TV personality and his relatively new wife, in the Concorde lounge in Terminal 5 as we were all having breakfast (I recommend the eggs Benedict, by the way). I appeared on his Radio 2 show last year and had quite a long and jolly conversation with him, but you can be sure that when someone is wearing sunglasses in the departure lounge they are not in the market for unsolicited approaches.

I was braving a transatlantic flight on BA for the first time in a while. Since my last experience, T5 has opened and the online check-in system has improved, so I was through the terminal in a flash and had time to spare to dispatch a BA person to find me a copy of the *FT* (a first-class airline lounge without the *FT*? I ask you). Even allowing for recent improvements, Heathrow and air travel in general have both become far less attractive than they were in my youth. Indeed, after the demise of Silverjet, the business-class-only airline I used to favour, I seriously thought about putting video-conferencing equipment in our office and cutting out air travel altogether. But there are some meetings for which only face-to-face will do, where you need to look someone in the eye and form your own judgment about them. And besides, you are very unlikely to enjoy an interesting chance meeting in a video conference.

So you can imagine my delight when, once onboard, I came face to face with an Oscar-nominated screenwriter in the seat to my left. Unfortunately, his first words to me were to explain that he was going to put up the privacy screen. Another rejection, though at least this time he spoke to me.

What is the etiquette for privacy screens? Should you ask the person next door if they mind you putting it up? And what to do if it turns out they do mind? What if you are married to them? But the screen went up, and I sat there worrying that I had developed body odour (or worse, halitosis), or that I maybe wasn't looking sufficiently glamorous or intellectual - unlikely, I know, but we should never rule things out simply for that reason. I examined my in-flight reading - the *FT*, *The Economist, Air Law* by Jeremy Pratt and The *PowerBook* by Jeanette Winterson. (This last I enjoyed very much, but why is it that I still feel slightly uncomfortable reading sex scenes written by someone I know?) I turned from the screenwriter to the person on my right. He was reading *L'Etranger* by Albert Camus, which made me feel even more inferior. Camus died in 1960, two years before I was born, so at least there's no danger of meeting him and then squirming in my seat while reading one of his sex scenes.

I was in California to present a paper at the Academy of Management conference. This was for some reason in Anaheim, a place where we took the two older Cost Centres once, many years ago, to visit Disneyland. If you are not going to Disneyland, or to a conference, don't go to Anaheim. I feel about this town as John Betjeman did about Slough - but even more depressing than Anaheim itself was the fact that more than 8,000 academics, all of whom teach management, were gathered there. This is twice the number that attended the last time I was at this conference, in 2000. Does the world need 8,000 teachers of management? Are we being managed twice as well as we were in 2000? I think not - businesses are just as likely as ever to fail, to hire bad people (or worse, hire good ones and fail to develop them), to expand inappropriately and so on.

The only improvement I detected since my last visit was a sharp drop in the incidence of facial hair among management academics. It has long been a source of irritation to me that academics tend towards beards. Surely they have more time to get busy with the razor than people who are actually managing something? But this year many more of them were clean-shaven - a definite improvement on 2000, as was the reception they

gave my paper (on the career trajectories of FTSE 100 CEOs).
Because the last time I submitted a paper to the Academy of
Management, it was rejected.

## FAINT HEARTS AND FAIR MAIDS
*Aug 30, 2008*

Cities are some of my favourite places. I am at my most
comfortable right in the heart of a city, being part of its energy,
watching the people. London, of course, is my favourite,
although I will admit to pangs of anxiety if I ever have to leave
the large-scale section of the A-Z map. When I sleep in my
bedroom at the office, I wake up to a Mary Poppins scene of the
rooftops of London and am reminded of the legions who live
and work within a few hundred metres of my front door.

With all those people in such a small area, you would think
that meeting people would be easy. But I still seem to have
a large entourage of eligible girlfriends who are attractive,
solvent, clever and great company, but for some unknown
reason remain unmarried and in many cases are not in a
relationship of any kind. And that doesn't just go for my
London girlfriends. Why is this? Where are all the men in these
cities? Don't they want girlfriends? Are they all married, or
homosexual, or just extraordinarily fussy?

Maybe cities are just too full of people who are all too busy to
embark on a meaningful relationship. But the countryside is no
better. I was intrigued when I visited the Game Fair at the end
of July to see that one of the most prominent stands was not for
a posh shotgun-maker such as Purdey or Holland & Holland,
but belonged to Muddy Matches, a rural dating agency.

The Lovely Lucinda is a prime example of a beautiful single
girl who would make someone a lovely girlfriend or even wife.
I have encouraged her to try the internet, and recently she even
paid (or, as regular readers will remember, persuaded her ex-
husband to pay) to join a dating agency that promptly sent her
out to meet several rather unsuitable men. She is not impressed
and informs me that the belly-dancing classes that she recently
started offer much better value for money – £135 for 12 lessons.
Are belly-dancing lessons likely to increase the number of men

she meets in London? I doubt it. I am also not sure that being a competent belly-dancer is on the list of most men's wants and needs when it comes to choosing a girlfriend or wife, but never mind. I have told her to lower her standards (of men, not of belly-dancing) and keep trying.

I was once asked, at a large career conference put on for women who worked in the City of London, what advice I would have for someone who was too busy doing 12-hour days on a trading floor to go out and find a boyfriend. Work fewer hours, obviously. But if you don't want to leave it to fate, seek a partner as you would an employee. Advertise (on the internet, or even in print if there is a publication that will take your advertisement and that you think like-minded souls will read), talk to anyone and everyone you meet, and – best of all – task your friends to seek out potential dates as though they were headhunters. Be braver! Be more direct! Don't fear rejection!

An eligible (if somewhat young) male who is about to tour several cities is Cost Centre #1, newly garlanded with three A grades at A-level. For those of you who live outside the UK, there are two things that you should know about this academic achievement. The first is that this is the best that he could have obtained, having only sat A-level examinations in three subjects. The second is that if he had not achieved these grades, given the amount of money and parental effort lavished on his education, I would have killed him.

He has joined the production crew of the stage play of *Alex*, a cartoon strip about an investment banker that appears in several newspapers around the world. He has the lowly job (quite right too) of being the "follow-spot" operator. He is therefore going to follow an actor on a stage with a spotlight in several cities, starting in Melbourne on September 10 and moving on to Sydney, Hong Kong, Singapore and Dubai. Lucky boy – they are all on my list of favourite cities.

## How new leaves affect turnover
*Sep 06, 2008*
Do plants belong in the workplace? The Lovely Lucinda arrived in the office today with a camera. Who was she going to

photograph? Quite a few good-looking men visit the office but even so, taking pictures of them might be a little excessive.

No, LL was going to walk down the street and photograph other people's window boxes. Why? Can't she think of something more useful to do with her time? Programming a few more numbers (the beauty therapist, the taxi company and the flying school) into my mobile phone? Getting the cracked window in the boardroom fixed? Or sorting out the loose carpet on the second-floor landing?

She was going to photograph other people's window boxes, she said, because they were so much better than ours and she wanted to work out why. Having a photographic record of these other, superior displays might allow her to upgrade our own efforts.

We have four window boxes, two at the front of the building and two at the back. I have never understood why we have them at the back. Who can see them? Our neighbours? Why are we investing time and money in improving our neighbours' utility? Jeremy Bentham would have had words to say on this.

My view is that plants are not necessary in an office. I asked Mr M if he has plants at work. I excluded Vitis vinifera (common grapevine), which, given his profession, is the only plant that he recognises, and which, strangely enough, his company grows around its building in suburban Berkshire. But indoor plants? He says they have "a few" although he barely notices them. I asked who waters them and he said he thought they had "an elderly lady" who did it, although he had never seen her.

Well, he won't be seeing her now, because he has resigned and left. This is not a frequent occurrence – since giving up the world of television for the world of wine, seven years ago, Mr M has only worked for two companies. He has just left an employer with less-than-memorable plants, but with whom he had negotiated an enviable arrangement involving a very generous amount of holiday for golf-related purposes. Instead, he has gone to work for Peter Jones. No, not the department store, the 41-year-old entrepreneur of Dragons' Den and

American Inventor fame. I have no idea whether Peter Jones has plants in his office – Mr M starts work there this Monday, so I look forward to finding out.

Mr M made the decision to go and work for Jones (and vice versa, I might add) very quickly and mainly on the basis of gut instinct. I made the decision to lease our office on the same basis and just as quickly. When I went to look round, it had been newly decorated and had window boxes at the front and two bay trees outside the front door. My colleagues were keen to keep the bay trees and the window boxes, and I couldn't be bothered to argue, so we did. We got in touch with the company that had supplied and maintained them while the building was being shown to prospective tenants, and they agreed to continue looking after them. On the mornings when our copies of the *FT* are sitting soaking wet on the doorstep, I know that everything has been watered.

Since we moved in, the bay trees and window boxes at the front have been supplemented by window boxes at the rear and more bay trees in the courtyard. (I have no recollection of signing a cheque for them.) These we maintain ourselves. LL has now decided that our response to the credit crunch must be to take over the maintenance of the window boxes at the front as well. This service costs us £720 a year, and to my mind is clearly discretionary spending, so I'm all for the change.

It will mean LL getting up very early twice a year, going via New Covent Garden to buy another load of plants and some soil, and then replanting the window boxes while trying not to make too much of a mess in the office. She will also stand to gain enviable topiary skills in her dealings with the bay trees. All very gratifying. But I can think of a much easier way to save £720. Get rid of the plants altogether.

## AT LAST, A PLACE FOR THE UNSUNG WAR HERO IN TRAFALGAR SQUARE
*Sep 13, 2008*

Anniversaries are important. I am usually good at remembering anniversaries, such as the first time I met anyone significant, the first time I did anything special (shot my first grouse, for example), the first time I got married (all right, I've only got married once, but you never know), the birthdays of my children, and the anniversary of the day that I led the management buyout of our company. We make a big fuss of anniversaries in our company; every year we present staff members with flowers (or, in the case of our very few boys, alcohol) on the anniversary of the day that they joined, and on all birthdays we have cake and read out a specially commissioned poem. With more than 20 people in the company, it is just as well that we have a few budding Tennysons or the poet laureate duties might prove rather a burden.

This weekend is the first anniversary of the only column I have ever written that has started a major campaign. On September 15 2007, I noticed that it was Battle of Britain day and offered my opinion that London was the poorer for not honouring the man who many believe did more to win the battle than anyone else. Sir Keith Park has many memorials to him in his home country of New Zealand, but for his inspired labours in the control room at RAF Uxbridge he was never given a permanent memorial in London. (I had not known that the control room was in Uxbridge, but I'm not surprised. Can any of you find Uxbridge on a map? Presumably they trusted in 1940 that neither could Hitler.)

After I wrote that column, a wealthy London-based businessman wrote to the FT offering to fund a statue to Sir Keith and started a campaign to have it placed on the fourth plinth in Trafalgar Square. This produced an outpouring of letters and e-mails to me, him and the paper from all over the world. Every party in the New Zealand parliament has given its support, as has the new Mayor of London, Boris Johnson, the MP for Westminster, Mark Field, and RAF boss Air Chief Marshal Sir Glenn Torpy. All these, together with the veterans' organisations and the Battle of Britain Historical Society, have helped the campaign (www.sirkeithpark.com).

This weekend, at the RAF Museum in Hendon, many people involved with the campaign meet to celebrate its success so far, and see a mock-up of the famous Uxbridge control room. On Saturday at 2pm, the businessman who launched the campaign with that letter to the FT will set out why Sir Keith should be remembered as one of Britain's greatest war heroes. Anyone can go along, and, if you feel like nipping over later, I can assure you that Hendon is much easier to find than Uxbridge.

The event is being supported by KEA, an organisation that unites New Zealanders living outside New Zealand (www. keanewzealand.com). Why do so many work overseas? After all, they have the most beautiful country in the world. Mind you, we should be grateful that New Zealanders do leave to work elsewhere - we might all be speaking German here if they didn't.

Which is why it is so pleasing that, a year on from my column, the Sir Keith Park Campaign has achieved what many said was impossible. Subject to planning approval by Westminster City Council, a statue of Sir Keith will be on the fourth plinth for six months from late autumn 2009. Thereafter, a permanent site will be found in a prestigious location nearby, the hope being that this will be in Waterloo Place. Seven sculptors are submitting designs and this month a committee will choose a winner. September 15 2010 will be the 70th anniversary of the Battle of Britain and this may be the last major anniversary where veterans of the battle still survive in any number. How nice, then, that the anniversary is expected to be marked by the dedication of the permanent statue. Thank you, everyone.

## WHY AM I BEING MADE TO SUBSIDISE MY CUSTOMERS?
*Sep 27 2008*

Business, rather than love, in a cold climate. In these straitened economic times the standard opening question on the drinks party circuit is: "How's business?" At one party in Mayfair recently, I found myself answering that question over and over again, finally giving up out of sheer boredom and heading for the exit just as most of the shadow cabinet bowled in. They all looked very chirpy, as if business was going very well for them. Which it is.

But if you are not a political party that has been in opposition for more than 11 years and can finally scent a kill, but instead you run a business operating in the UK, there is less to smirk about. Our firm is just as busy as it was, I found myself repeating that night, but the work we have to do to service that business has more than doubled. In addition, clients are increasingly looking to fund their working capital from the cheapest source – their suppliers.

We are a small firm – a very small firm – and our clients are almost all huge. Yet they are treating us like a bank, and they're not asking us whether we want to play that role. We are currently providing more than 60 days' credit for several vast international companies that, in my opinion, should be using more appropriate organisations (ie banks) to fund their working capital.

So why don't we do the same? We don't have major suppliers. If I decided not to pay the stationery supplier for 60 days, it would have an almost imperceptible impact on our cost of capital and would probably ensure that our supply of pencils was cut off. Our biggest input, like many companies in the Great British service economy, is people. And I can't suddenly decide not to pay the wages for 60 days.

This recession seems to be different, somehow. Its casualties appear mostly to be very prominent and are well-known names. Lehman Brothers may be hogging the headlines, but for many in the UK, the casualty of the year has to be Wrapit, the wedding-list company.

Our office will see two weddings this year. In March my only Luxembourg-born employee married a very posh builder and followed my example by not having a traditional wedding cake. They had cup cakes – Mr M and I, 20 years ago, had a croquembouche. My other employee marrying this year (also with continental origins, this time Spanish) is spurning not only a traditional wedding cake but a traditional wedding, and going off to Las Vegas to be married by Elvis. Go girl!

Wrapit was very popular with the English middle classes and seems to have lived off the generosity of its clients' friends.

Wedding presents purchased months in advance did not need to
be delivered until after the day. Wrapit also held back payment
from suppliers, so it was cheap working capital all round – until
the house came tumbling down, leaving not only my employee
but also Holly the Sadist, my personal trainer, who was married
in August, owed lots of wedding presents she will never see.
My Most Socially Acceptable Girlfriend claims that Harrods is
the best place to have your wedding list, because it is prepared
to hand you up to one-third of your list's value in cash, instead
of gifts. So when Aunt Harriet calls in and buys you that cut-
glass decanter that you have always wanted, you add another
one to the list knowing that even if four people buy it, you can
take delivery of one and cash for the rest, or buy something that
you really want instead. The chance of all four decanter-donors
coming to dinner at once is pretty remote, one hopes.

And our working capital? This year our most senior staff,
including me, have had to accept their bonuses in three
instalments. So now the employees are banking the company.
Another subject for drinks parties.

## THINGS HAVE CHANGED AROUND HERE: TREAD CAREFULLY, MR M...
*Oct 04 2008*

Change is stressful. Starting a new job, moving house and
divorce are often cited as three of the most common causes
of stress. Mr M and I are not contemplating divorce, but he
has just changed job in the same week that we completed the
purchase of our new house and moved in.

Yes, the Moneypenny family has purchased a property – in
the worst housing market for a long while. For the past eight
years we have been renting, while we put our capital to other
uses. Renting made sense for several reasons, but the whole
Moneypenny family had become rather bored of never being
able to improve or modify the home because to do so would
simply add value to someone else's property. So we have
bought our own, and we think we have benefited from the dire
state of the housing market, not least because we have no plans

to sell it for many, many years – at least until Cost Centre #3 (now aged nine) has left university, if then.

We have not been able to move our cricket net, but given that a gate leads directly from our back garden on to the village cricket pitch, complete with its own nets, it hardly seemed necessary to have our own as well. However, we do plan to construct a golf net instead.

Mr M took three weeks off between jobs. We used the time to prepare for our move and to go away together for 24 hours. This might seem a little perfunctory for a holiday, especially an overseas one, but we went to Bruges. Keen-eyed readers will note that Bruges begins with a "b", as do the adjectives "beautiful" and "boring", both of which can be appropriately used in this context. Twenty-four hours is long enough for a visit to Bruges, I can assure you.

Before the start of his new job, as an early birthday present, I said that I would arrange for Mr M to go for two days of intensive golf coaching at the David Leadbetter Golf Academy. The DLGA is based in the US but it has one UK branch, which happens to be eight miles from Middlesbrough and 207 miles from where we live. Why? And why is there only one in the UK? They have six in France! I called up and asked when they had availability. In the whole of Mr M's three weeks off, they had only two days available – the two days of the house move.

After calming down and thinking about it, I decided that it was still for the best. How helpful are husbands during a house move anyway? They only interfere and stop you from throwing away all their junk. So the night before the move Mr M set off for the north-east and spent two days on the golf course.

I, on the other hand, spent two days putting stuff into boxes, filling three skips, opening boxes at the other end, finding light bulbs, coffee and tea towels when no one could remember where they were packed, agonising over furniture that did not fit into its intended destination, making sure that CC#2's bedroom was repainted from Barbie-doll pink to magnolia before he came home from boarding school and threw a fit, making sure that the dog did not escape ... and so on.

In the new house Mr M has his own annexe with his hundreds (literally) of books on sport, a plasma-screen TV and a glass cabinet awaiting future golf trophies. Plus his wine collection, wine-storage cabinet and all his wine books. All of this was unpacked and sorted out so that he could arrive back and find it in situ. I even arranged for someone to come and connect the satellite TV box, and made our bed up with fresh linen. So when he returned, the house was well on the way, and his sports annexe, his bedroom and the kitchen were all ready to receive him. I had even made a delicious dinner.

What was the first thing he said? "Have you moved over the Setanta subscription?" That's another TV sports service, for the poor innocents among you. Maybe I should reconsider what I said about not planning on divorce.

## THE FINANCIAL COLLAPSE AND OTHER CAUSES FOR CONCERN
*Oct 11, 2008*
Go on, you try. You try to get anyone's attention for worthy causes while the financial world is collapsing around us. Nearly 600,000 women might die in childbirth each year but if a bank is going bust almost every day, it is tough to get anyone to notice.

Fortunately, for those unlucky enough to live in parts of the world where childbirth is routinely life-threatening, people do keep trying. Following on from the Davos dinner in January, when 40 important and influential women (OK, 39 and me) met to discuss Millennium Development Goal 5 (to reduce maternal mortality), a ladies' lunch was held in London in March by Sarah Brown and Carla Bruni. It was in support of the White Ribbon Alliance for Safe Motherhood (WRA), an international coalition that seeks to make childbirth safer. Last month, a larger WRA ladies-only dinner was held in New York. Wendi Murdoch, who with Queen Rania of Jordan and Indra Nooyi, CEO of PepsiCo, had hosted the original Davos dinner, put immense energy and effort into staging the New York event, and this time her co-hosts were Queen Rania and Brown.

The Lovely Lucinda asked me what I was going to wear to the dinner. I explained that it didn't really matter – I was going to be the least consequential person there. Just to prove this, I flew across the Atlantic with my fellow guests Elle Macpherson and Sarah Ferguson. If you ever wish to feel inconsequential, may I recommend a seven-hours-hour plane journey in the company of a supermodel and a former royal wife who spends almost all her time on philanthropy.

We were joined on the Manchester-NY leg of the journey by political hacks en route to cover the prime minister's visit to the UN special session. I got chatting to them and asked if they would like to meet Elle. With one exception, they all said yes. The exception did not decline, but asked who Elle Macpherson was. Who is Elle Macpherson? I could have forgiven this from an Oxbridge-educated journalist from a worthy newspaper, but not when this person's sister is a (very) famous fashion editor.

The dinner was held at a restaurant called Tao, which I am sure had never seen anything like it. I fought my way through the door amid a tide of media people, a consequence of arriving just behind Sarah Palin. Right now, even people who don't know who Elle Macpherson is have heard of Sarah Palin. My dinner companion was Martha Stewart. This proved handy when trying to establish what to do with empty edamame pods. The worry about which receptacle to choose was hardly in the same league as the question over what to do about the fact that Millennium Development Goal 5 is the only one that has not come closer to being achieved, but at least Stewart was there to help me. We discussed, inter alia, the financial crisis, our respective Agas (hers is grey with four ovens, mine red with two) and maternal mortality.

By bringing together Stewart, along with 99 of the most powerful and influential women in New York that week (the guests ranged from Susie Buffett to Vera Wang, as well as a few first ladies to support our own) it was hoped that a swelling tide of indignation about the lack of progress in achieving Millennium Development Goal 5 would lead to a greater sustained effort on the part of world leaders to redouble their efforts to get there.

Brown, Murdoch and Queen Rania had assembled an impressive guest list, even as Washington was striving to reach an agreement on a rescue fund for the US financial system. Banks will stand and fall, and it is right that our governments should act to solve the current crisis that is grabbing all the headlines. Although, if you are bleeding to death after childbirth in sub-Saharan Africa, I doubt that you will notice.

## LET ME PUT THIS DIPLOMATICALLY. BE NICE OR BELT UP
*Oct 25, 2008*
Diplomacy, according to an unattributed quote, is thinking twice before saying nothing. I fancied myself as a diplomat once. I can't imagine why, since I have - more than most people - a tendency to say the wrong thing at the wrong moment. But I sat the civil service exams while at university and it is a testament to the rigour of the British government's selection process that it rejected me.

I do make an effort, however, not to offend. It is a skill that I have not mastered completely - and neither have quite a few others, from the top to the bottom. I had breakfast not long ago with the chief executive of a large company who is a big pin-up of mine. (No, this is not diplomatic speak, or even more gushing drivel, but a genuine description. I do think he is very handsome, and he is in his late fifties: the perfect age for a man.) We both fly (at least, he flies - I am merely learning) and were discussing our aviation medicals. I shared the sorry tale of how I only just passed mine because I'm so fat.

Now, for the benefit of any male readers, let me explain something. When you are out on a breakfast date with a lady who expresses depression about her weight, you are supposed to say something like: "There, there, Mrs M, don't worry, you look gorgeous as you are," or, "I'm honoured to be seen in a prominent place having breakfast with you," or even, "Those eggs and bacon are very low calorie really," for example. What he actually said was: "Why don't you go on a diet?" and then, before I could recover from the shock and respond, he added:

"My secretary has, and she's lost three stone."

I related this tale a week later to one of his senior executive team. She did not say anything diplomatic either. She sent me the weblink to a diet website! I briefly glanced at it. It had an interactive section where you could calculate your Body Mass Index, complete with a silhouette of a perfectly proportioned lady. To check my doctor's figures, I entered my height and weight. To my horror, not only did the website tell me that my BMI was a number that I cannot possibly divulge, but the silhouette immediately changed to represent the proportions of the body in question - so it shrunk in height and expanded in circumference. Grotesque. This experience did not persuade me to try the diet. Rather, I arranged to have the site blocked for all users in my office.

Back at work, at our regular Monday staff meeting, I related my aviation triumph of the weekend, namely passing my Air Law exam with 85 per cent. Present was our newest and most junior member of the team, a graduate trainee who is all of 22 and a qualified helicopter pilot. Her degree is in politics, which is surely close to diplomacy. Asked by me, in front of many of the team, what she had got in her Air Law exam, she honestly replied 87 per cent. She will clearly go far. Anyone else might have invented a lower mark to make me look good. Showing up the boss in your first week at work demonstrates potential.

My most recent encounter with a diplomat, however, was when I took a potential client out to dinner. I was at my charming best, the restaurant was lovely and he was fascinating. We discussed his recent deer-stalking successes in Scotland, and I told him that, until recently, I had stayed away from stalking as I thought it sounded too much like hard work - all that walking, mostly into the wind and uphill, carrying a rifle. But I have finally been persuaded to give it a try, and will be stalking fallow deer in Ireland next month.

As I said goodbye to this prospective client after an excellent Thai meal, I could see him looking at me and could tell he was wondering whether to say what was going through his head. "Enjoy the stalking," was his farewell remark. "But if I were you, I'd get on the treadmill."

## WOMEN BANKERS: CREDIT WHERE IT'S DUE
*Nov 01, 2008*

More women, better banks? This is the theory currently being advanced. Of course, there are plenty of women in banking, especially retail banking. I suspect half the workforce of Britain's retail banks are female. A career as a bank teller is one that sits supportively with family life. But women in charge of a bank? There are very few.

Gail Kelly is one of them, and she is the chief executive of Westpac. She was previously the CEO of St George, a far smaller bank in Australia. When she arrived at Westpac she promptly bid for St George, a deal that shareholders will vote on this month. That's decisive action for you. One of Kelly's strengths is that a long time ago, in her native South Africa, she taught Latin. Remember my colleague Gillian Tett mentioning that the word credit was derived from the Latin for "I trust"? Latin teaching is a great background for a banker.

In Iceland, I am delighted that they have put women in charge of cleaning up the mess. Elin Sigfusdottir and Birna Einarsdottir have been appointed the chief executives of New Landsbanki and New Glitnir respectively, the nationalised banks created by the Icelandic government in the wake of the financial crisis. Where did they get them from? Iceland, a country with a population roughly the size of Doncaster, surely doesn't have cupboards full of female bankers waiting around for things to go wrong. The two women were both promoted from inside the banks that failed. Sigfusdottir has been head of corporate banking at Landsbanki since 2003 and Einarsdottir became head of domestic commercial banking at Glitnir last summer. (Thank goodness for modern word processors or I would never have got those names right.) The *FT* reported that the two women were "expected to curb the bonus-driven risk-taking culture that has taken hold in Iceland over the past five years".

Now, let's get one thing straight here. I don't believe that bonuses are a flawed compensation model. Surely any model that minimises fixed costs is a good one in troubled times. No, the problem with bonuses is that people have come to regard them as a given. Bonus is derived from the Latin for "good" - in other words a bonus is a treat. It should not be taken for granted. Back in Iceland, as I have mentioned, women are in charge of two of the three failed banks. But what about Kaupthing? There's a woman in charge of that, too, at least in the UK. Ernst & Young have been appointed receivers to Kaupthing and the letter that I have just received telling me that our company - as a wholesale depositor - is an unsecured creditor, is signed by three people, one of whom is a woman.

Why are we unsecured creditors of Kaupthing? It's a very unfortunate story, and it doesn't involve me being the gullible treasurer of a UK local authority. My management buyout was financed by Singer & Friedlander, who were subsequently bought by Kaupthing. As I have written before, we closed our account with Kaupthing in April and retreated to Arbuthnot, a very boring UK bank run by a Swiss proprietor who doesn't finance his bank from the wholesale money market. But some clients do not read their invoices correctly, and lo! We suddenly found that a client had paid a substantial sum into our old bank.

Am I worried? No. Why? Because a woman is in charge. Maggie Mills is a corporate restructuring partner who has been coping with this kind of chaos since 1979, so she must be a bit older than me. Maggie is the (wait for this, we clearly have title inflation) "Global Coordinating Partner" for Ernst & Young's restructuring practices. She impressed everyone when she worked on Baring, some 13 years ago, so I have every faith in her dealing with Kaupthing. Women running banks? Bring it on.

## TUMBLING MARKETS - AND STUMBLING COLUMNISTS
*Nov 08, 2008*

Badly bruised shins. Not the souvenir you expect from Dubai, but that's what I came home with. Other people return with a tan, or a piece of jewellery acquired in a souk, or even just a photograph of the Burj, but me? I am purple from knee to ankle on both legs.

I was in Dubai on business, and would anyway not be looking to come home with a tan since I avoid the sun (at my age you don't want to soak up too many rays, or 46 can quickly turn into 64). No, I was planning to develop new relationships for my business and bring back a freshly stocked contacts book. I was also hoping to bring back Cost Centre #1's university application form, since he was there too, briefly, as part of his world travels. I managed both of those – but also the brightly coloured shins.

I blame it on my editor. He was also in Dubai for a (very) brief visit to meet some of the key movers and shakers, and to hear at first hand how the Middle East is faring in the credit shock. He kindly invited me to join him and the *FT*'s local staff for dinner, at the Atlantis hotel.

Now, for those of you unfamiliar with the Atlantis, here are a few facts. It opened as recently as late September; it is built at the end of the first (and so far only completed) Dubai Palm, a piece of reclaimed land designed to resemble a palm tree; it has more than 1,500 rooms; it has a theme park next door so you could show up there and never leave, especially as it also contains a branch of Nobu and every shop you might require; and it has a mammoth aquarium built into the centre of its east wing. Add to this the fact that the weather in Dubai rarely disappoints and you can see why their presidential suite has been booked solid since opening.

Dubai traffic being what it is, I arrived a little late. I called my editor to see where he was. His text message said he was being shown the hotel by its boss, who I presumed to be the general manager. I set off to join him in the east wing, where he and a small group of *FT* colleagues and local *FT* readers were being shown the Neptune suite.

The hotel blurb describes it thus: "Stretching over three floors, the Neptune Suite welcomes guests with a grand foyer leading down a sweeping staircase into an elegant aquatic-themed dining and living area, with butler's pantry. Then, of course, there are the sumptuous bed and bathrooms with their underwater views.

If guests are unable to tear themselves away from watching the 65,000 marine animals, a 24-hour dedicated private butler is available to serve refreshments."

I was met at the door and escorted down the "sweeping staircase". Just then two things struck me.

One was that the 65,000 marine animals were mesmerising. And the other was that it was not the general manager showing my editor the hotel. It was the founder and chairman of Dubai World, the ultimate holding company behind the Atlantis and the Dubai Palm itself. At that point on the sweeping staircase, I was swept off my feet. I lost my footing and plunged down the remaining stairs, landing in a heap at the feet of His Excellency Sultan Ahmed bin Sulayem.

For all I know, this is the correct way to greet Emirati billionaires, but just in case it wasn't, I leapt up – shins in agony – and offered him my hand to shake instead. It is a measure of his calm and composure that he seemed to treat overweight, middle-aged columnists throwing themselves at his feet as though it were an everyday occurrence.

My editor, though, turned ashen, while Cost Centre #1 (who was behind me) said afterwards that it was the most embarrassing moment of his life so far (there is competition for that honour).

Dubai World is developing the world's tallest building, the Nakheel Tower, which will have 200 floors. So that's a lot more steps to fall down, then. I shall return to Dubai when my shins heal.

### NEVER SO GLAD TO BE STOOD UP, I TOOK OFF
*Nov 15, 2008*

Thank you, Vivian Fernandez de Torrijos. We have never met, but I want to let you know how grateful I am. If it weren't for you, I would still be waiting to make my first solo flight.

I have wanted to meet the First Lady of Panama even longer than I have wanted to take the controls of an aeroplane without an instructor beside me. I have always thought that Senõra Fernandez de Torrijos looked like suitable Girlfriend material:

our birthdays are two days apart (although she is four years younger); she is thinner and prettier than me (not so difficult, I grant you); she's a powerhouse of energy and seemingly capable of doing 1,001 things at once as well as raising three children, one of whom is disabled. (It also turns out that her two boys are named after their father and grandfather, a convention I too have followed.) And on top of all this she is married to the president of a country that controls of one of the world's most important waterways, which runs right through the middle of the place.

Without wanting to sound like a stalker, I did get close to her recently. She was at a dinner for high-powered women (and me) in New York to raise awareness of maternal mortality, at the same table as Sarah Brown, the media-shy wife of our prime minister. So was Susan Buffett. (A reader wrote in after I first reported this dinner to say that she knew I was a name-dropper, but now she knew I was making it up – Susan Buffett died in 2004. Well, this was Susan Alice Buffett, her daughter. And I never make anything up.)

Needless to say, I was seated miles from this august table and never managed to greet Vivian, let alone tell her that I hoped she would become my Panamanian Girlfriend.

Presumably, putting her next to Margaret Chan, director-general of the World Health Organisation, would have allowed the two of them to discuss Vivian's initiatives to improve female health in her country. But I am a trustee of a big educational charity, and she's doing a lot for education in Panama, so we too would have had something to talk about. But the chance never came.

So I was pleased to be invited to breakfast with her during a planned visit to London. Sadly, she had to postpone the trip and so I found myself short of a breakfast date on a day with glorious weather – Wednesday, October 29. And for once, the crosswinds that had prevented me from taking my first solo flight had eased.

I made a beeline for Oxford Airport and Richard, my flying instructor. The winds were described as "light and variable".

Richard is a lot lighter than me though not at all variable
– he invariably talks non-stop, firing a constant barrage of
instructions at me. (I know I have said this before, but what is
it about men and giving instructions, be it flying, golf or most
other activities? If they gave that many directions in bed, we
would all be better off.)

Three circuits later, as we landed, Richard announced to
air traffic control that he was going to send me up alone. My
whoop of joy was heard all the way to Brize Norton.

Off I went, and it was not without incident. I came in to land
too high and couldn't get the aeroplane down correctly. So, as
I knew I should, I opened the throttle and went up again. The
plane was horribly sluggish and I struggled to get it to speed up.
It was only on the downwind leg that I realised I still had the
flaps extended. For those of you unfamiliar with aviation, I had
in effect driven round the block with the handbrake on.

I landed, at the second attempt, perfectly. "Congratulations,"
said air traffic control, "two for the price of one." So now I am
on the way to my pilot's licence, and I might need it if I am ever
to meet Vivian. There are no direct flights to Panama from the
UK. I'll have to fly there myself.

## WHO SAYS THERE'S NO ROMANCE IN HATFIELD
*Nov 22, 2008*

Do you write poetry? I used to, in my youth, but I've almost
completely given up in favour of prose since reaching the age
of 21, and have only broken this habit in moments of serious
emotional turmoil. The last poem I wrote was in January 2005.

One of my more romantic friends (and a former editor of
The Sun) wrote a poem recently. It was a love poem, and just
to make sure that the object of his affections didn't miss it,
he had it published in a magazine. Not just any magazine, but
The *Spectator*. How mad was that? According to the Speccy's
website, it has a circulation of about 80,000, the average reader
is 58 and has a net worth of £1m. So if his poem stirs them,
my romantic friend could well find himself with some serious
competition from people older and wealthier than him.

He invited me to a dinner a few days after publication (no, I was not the intended subject of his poem), and I went along expecting to sit next to someone aged 58 with a net worth of £1m. Instead, I sat next to Tim Steiner, CEO of the online grocery delivery company Ocado. He is 38, and judging by the value placed on the business when the John Lewis Partnership transferred its stake in Ocado to its pension fund the other day, Tim is worth a great deal more than £1m.

I already knew all about Ocado, and not just because I am a customer. You would have to have been living in a cave these past few years not to know how Mr Steiner and his former colleagues from Goldman Sachs started out in one room in 2000 and now, having developed some very clever information technology, have 20 per cent of the online grocery market in Britain and a high-tech distribution centre where 12,000 orders are picked every day.

What I didn't know is that the 23-acre site of this grocery revolution is built on part of the runway of the former Hatfield Aerodrome, originally the home of the de Havilland Aircraft Company. The de Havilland Comet was the world's first commercial jet airliner to reach production, and first flew in 1949. Early models had big problems with air pressures and damage to their shells, and so a test chamber was built (partly underground, mainly over) to test aircraft in simulated conditions of 70,000ft altitude, and -70°C. It sat right opposite where Ocado is now. The test hangar is the largest aluminium building in Europe, is listed, and is now a gym.

Before developers got their hands on Hatfield (when British Aerospace, the successor company to de Havilland, sold it), Stephen Spielberg filmed *Saving Private Ryan* and *Band Of Brothers* there.

But possibly the most interesting person associated with the aerodrome was Eddie Chapman, a double agent in the Second World War who, having been recruited by the Germans when they found him in prison in the Channel Islands, was dispatched to England to commit acts of sabotage. Captured by British forces, he then changed sides and helped stage a fake attack on his target at Hatfield, where the Mosquito was built. It was so realistic (MI5 conjured up a false news story with the Daily Express to lend credibility to the raid) that the Germans were fooled and he returned to Germany to spy for Britain for the rest of the war.

But Chapman was a double agent in other areas, too. He managed to have, at the same time, two wartime fiancées, one in England (Freda Stevenson) and one in German-occupied Norway (Dagmar Lahlum). Which one did he marry? Neither. After the war, he abandoned them both and instead married his prewar lover Betty Farmer. If he was looking for emotional turmoil, he found it in spades. I bet that generated some poetry.

## A FEW FESTIVE SUGGESTIONS – AND NONE OF THEM EXTRAVAGANT
*Nov 29, 2008*

It's that time of the year again. Yes, Christmas is approaching. This is probably the most stressful season for many marriages, including my own. It is not for nothing that I keep divorce lawyer Diane Benussi's book *How Not To Get Divorced After Christmas* on my desk. (This, by the way, can be downloaded for free from the internet, and includes a very helpful section – I'm told – on how to conduct yourself over Christmas if you are having an affair. Personally, I don't see how anyone these days can possibly find time.)

The reason Christmas is stressful for me is not because we are off to spend it in Australia with my in-laws. No, the stress arises from the need to exchange gifts. In particular, Mr M is charged with giving me a gift, which he finds an unusually onerous responsibility.

He says that I am very difficult to buy for because he has no idea what I might want/need. So this year I took pity on him and flagged up in about June the gift that I would most like – a gift, moreover, that would not take up much room on our trip to the southern hemisphere. I am not big on family photos on the desk, so to make sure I think of the Cost Centres every minute of the day I wear bracelets decorated with their initials. Or, to be more accurate, I wear two – one with CC#2's initial and one with CC#3's initial. They are called Hakka bracelets and are made by Cassandra Goad – I am only being so explicit about this because of the tedious frequency of the questions I have had from Mr M on the subject since I first brought it up. Yes, I would like one with CC#1's initial. Yes, his initial is R. Yes, you can buy them online. Yes, as we enter a recession, I would like it in silver rather than gold. By the time I have finished the questionnaire, I might as well have bought it myself.

I am clearly not the only person that has this problem – when I went on to the website for the first time to check what the bracelet was called, I noticed that the site has a "send a hint" button.

I did in the end complain about the barrage of questions from Mr M and suggested that it took something of the magic out of present-giving. This caused a testy exchange of e-mails, the final one of which was entitled "Presents I have enjoyed". Here is Mr M's list: "golf clothes (wet weather stuff, inner clothing), special golf gloves, Titleist NXT golf balls, clothes, trips…"

Is it necessary to be so specific? Even the *Financial Times* is getting in on the act. This year we all received an e-mail entitled "Christmas Presents", outlining procedures for dealing with gifts or hospitality considered to be "overly extravagant". What is "overly extravagant" at the *FT*? Five hundred pounds, it turns out. I am instructed that all corporate hospitality worth more than £500 should be "politely declined". No wonder I never meet any *FT* journalists shooting. Also, all gifts with a value of more than £500 must be "declined" (although we are not instructed to do so politely) or donated to charity. Thank goodness times are so bad that a six-bottle case of Krug is being offered online for less than £500. (Although *FT* gifts between £50 and £500 have to be declined as well, they are not considered extravagant.)

So then, for future reference, Mr M, here we go – all under £500 and thus not extravagant. Pashminas of any colour, 24 Faubourg by Hermès, white chocolate, any jewellery other than rings, anything from Jo Malone other than scented candles,

Moleskine notebooks, nice pens and pencils, and gift certificates for the new waxing salon in Davies Street, Mayfair. After 20 years of marriage you wouldn't think this was necessary – 20 years on December 28, as it happens. Another present-buying opportunity.

## OF SONS AND MOTHERS
*Dec 06, 2008*

Have you raised an equal opportunity household? I am not sure that I have. All three Cost Centres seem reluctant to engage with domestic machinery – dishwasher, washing machine and vacuum cleaner are three that come to mind.

Not that CC#1 is troubling me very much at the moment, since he is away on his gap year in Australia. He is currently in Melbourne working in what the Australians call a bottle shop and we in the UK call an off-licence. I am not sure what he is learning there, if anything, although he may well be exposed to an equal opportunity household. The wife of the bottle-shop owner is a noted business development adviser to many of Australia's top law and accountancy firms and has just published her first book, *Growing Your Professional Practice*. I am sure that everyone in her house can operate the domestic appliances.

Australian women are to be found working in senior positions all over the place. My Airline Girlfriend, for instance, is Australian and runs all the training for a large airline based in the Middle East that draws its cabin crew from more than 100 nationalities. It's a big job, especially when you consider that the airline concerned employs 10,000 cabin crew.

Australian women are working in such large numbers in the UK nowadays that there is even an annual award for the most prominent. But I was startled to discover that they are not the only foreigners who can win prizes. Last month I was invited to the "Français of the year" presentation, for goodness sake. These awards "celebrate the most talented French people who live and work in the UK". I didn't go. (I am not averse to all things French, and indeed wear a French version of the Wellington boot, but I had a prior engagement.) I did scour the shortlist and am not sure that many of them could really be described as French, given how long they have lived and worked in the UK. Michel Roux Jnr? Nicole Farhi?

CC#1 is not sure what nationality he is, since he carries both UK and Australian passports, as do his brothers. He was in Dubai a couple of months ago and was stranded there because all the flights to Melbourne were full. He spent his days at the home of AG, waiting to get a seat, and to relieve his boredom she took him to work one day. (Why was he bored? Being in Dubai with decent weather, a pool and an endless supply of books sounds blissful to me.) At AG's work, he got to experience a simulated forced landing, which required him to evacuate the aircraft by chute, and then he spent a few hours playing a disgruntled passenger in the first-class training cabin of the A380. Three of these aircraft are already in service with the airline concerned, with many more on order, hence the need for training. CC#1 ate meal after meal after meal. His most challenging moment of this experience? Being served coffee by all five staff, one at a time. It was of the very strong, Turkish variety, and by the time he had finished he was wired. It was only then that he noticed they had given him a bucket to pour them away.

I was very grateful to AG for housing and feeding CC#1 until he could escape to Melbourne. But on reflection, I am not sure that I am so pleased about the A380 experience. I (like many mothers) have not helped him become an equal opportunity thinker – instead, I have produced food, done laundry and helped solve quadratic equations where necessary. To my shame, I find that I am repeating the exercise (including the quadratic equations) for CC#2. Will putting a spoilt middle-class teenager in a very comfortable seat with unlimited access to TV and music channels, and then sending a stream of attractive women to wait on him, do much to improve matters?

## ON THE PERILS OF SPEAKING WITHOUT NOTES
*Dec 13, 2008*
I am rarely nervous. Sure, there is always the occasional client that I have to work myself up to speak to, and every now

and then a piece of bad news that I am apprehensive about delivering. But it takes a lot to make me really nervous. Sitting on the runway waiting to take off for my first solo flight, I was very nervous. But it's not a regular feature in my emotional repertoire.

So when I had to speak in front of a large audience at the Barbican the other day, I should have taken it in my stride. I was there to receive an honorary degree, which itself is a slightly nerve-racking experience. I was not alone – there was another recipient, Don Lewin. We sat on the platform together while 500 students received their degrees, and then we, in turn, received ours.

The procedure for this is that the person to be honoured stands up while someone from the university reads a citation. This is very like listening to your own obituary. Then the chancellor places your hood and hat on you (your sizes of gown and hat having been e-mailed to the university in advance). As I already have a doctorate, I knew what the hat looked like – more like something out of Tudor times than a mortar-board. Next you move to the lectern to speak for about five minutes. Finally, a second batch of 500 students receive their degrees.

I had not prepared my speech. I am not good at delivering prepared speeches, and the most I will ever do is to jot some notes down on the back of an envelope. But, finding myself facing 2,000 people, I started to feel a bit nervous. What was I going to say? I needed a killer opening line, and just couldn't think of one, even after the procession of the first 500 students had finished. Then came the citation for Don Lewin.

Born the son of a chimney sweep in east London 75 years ago, he was working by the age of 10, and when he left school was determined not to sweep chimneys. He wanted a greetings card shop and, while saving up for one, he sold cards from the boot of his car and vacuum cleaners door-to-door. Eventually he got the shop, and now has many more of them. He took his company, Clinton Cards, public 20 years ago and today employs 10,000 people, including his son and daughter. The citation mentioned that at a very early stage in his career he realised a childhood dream of buying a Rolls-Royce – for cash. He has also been at the forefront of innovation, putting divorce cards in his shops before anyone else in the UK, and, more recently, redundancy cards, which I imagine might be a best-selling item in the weeks and months to come.

Mr Lewin had prepared his speech, and it contained some good advice for the graduating students. "There are 24 hours in a day," he said. "Use them." Then he reminded us of the phrase: "Six hours' sleep for men, seven for women, more for fools." After the list of his achievements, his authentic rags-to-riches story and then his common-sense words for the audience, I was really worried. How was I going to follow that? I had still not thought of the killer opening line. I stood and listened to my own obituary, all the while trying to decide what to say.

Then the chancellor stood in front of me and placed the hat on my head. But as he put it on, I realised that it was several sizes too small and balanced precariously on my head like a very thin book. The chancellor made reference to the size of my head and then invited me to give my speech.

If I had taken a single step the hat would have fallen off. Instead, I took it off, walked to the lectern and delivered my opening line: "That's what happens when your secretary decides to guess your hat size."

Here, at last, was my killer opening line. The person I am going to kill is the Lovely Lucinda. She's the one who should be really nervous.

## THE DAY I ACQUIRED A ONE-WAY TICKET TO STRESSVILLE
*Dec 20, 2008*

Rest and recuperation. That's what I shall be trying to achieve over the Christmas and New Year break. No matter that I have to travel commercial – and worse, economy – all the way to Australia to spend Christmas with my in-laws. Once there I shall go to sleep for a week.

I'll need the break. It just so happens that it is four years to the day since we completed the buyout of our company, and there has been plenty of stress since we embarked on that journey.

But which was worst? The near-collapse of the economy and the disappearance of large sums of our cash into a black hole called Kaupthing Singer & Friedlander? No. The worst in recent memory was my trip to the Passport Office.

Cost Centre #3 needed a new passport: a new British passport. Like his brothers, he has both UK and Australian citizenship. This is a nightmare, as in both countries children's passports are valid for only five years, which means we have six different passport dates and six different renewal opportunities. Mr M is now trying to add to the chaos by himself applying for a British passport. Having passed the citizenship exam, Life in the UK, and correctly guessed how many Catholics there are in the country and where one might hear a Geordie accent, he has handed over £600 or so and we wait.

CC#3, however, could not wait. Three weeks ago the Lovely Lucinda pointed out that his UK passport expires on December 27. We could go to Australia, but CC#3 would not be accompanying us back. So LL booked me a special interview at the Passport Office and I filled out a form.

I sent it for countersigning to my Lawyer Friend, who has known Mr M and me since we were newly married and is familiar with all three Cost Centres. As a renowned parliamentary lawyer, he is a partner at a firm within spitting distance of Parliament Square, so not a million miles from the Passport Office. I arranged to collect the form the following morning.

Stupidly, I had not heeded the date: Wednesday, December 3 – the state opening of Parliament. This is an archaic ritual for which the Queen dresses up as though she were attending a party thrown by Elton John (tiara, white fur) and then goes to the House of Lords to read a speech which the government has written for her, detailing the planned legislation for the coming year. Hardly a laugh a minute. Everyone dresses up to listen to her – even though she reads in a monotone (I've no idea why, perhaps she worries in case she's seen to favour any particular bill. Nor can I see HM seeking to take advantage of the new flexible working arrangements outlined in her speech – she has worked non-stop since she was a girl, and only took a break between two batches of children because she had to start a new job when a vacancy arose for a monarch.)

Bearing this event in mind, you might agree that possibly the stupidest place to send a passport form that you need back on the morning of the state opening of Parliament is to a parliamentary lawyer based in Westminster. I could not get within a mile of his office by cab. In the end, I resorted to running there – fighting my way past all the policemen to get down the road to his office – and then running back again. I arrived at the Passport Office fit to expire, which became even more imminent when I found I had to hand over £94.

That evening, to de-stress, I went to watch the Barbarians v Australia rugby match, as a guest of my Banker Girlfriend. BG runs the retail arm of a Very Large Bank which is shortly to become Even Larger. I loved the new Wembley stadium (built, as it happens, by an Australian construction firm), but we both froze. So I'm off to Australia, where I can rest and recuperate in the warm. It's a far better climate for watching rugby, too. Merry Christmas!

## THE GOOD, THE BAD AND THE FRANKLY UNFORGIVABLE
*Dec 27, 2008*

How was 2008 for you? It's bound to go down in the history books as a big year, not least thanks to the economy. But for me, each year is framed in terms of the people – because it is people who make things happen.

So: my heroes and villains for 2008.

I will probably never know the names of many of my villains. Which idiot in the Treasury thought up the idea of a one-size-fits-all capital gains tax? One of the most invigorating decisions of our prime minister when he was chancellor was to reduce the tax paid by entrepreneurs, to a minimum of 10 per cent (known in the UK as taper relief). It inspired many of us to risk money, time and a lot of effort to create new jobs. Now that there is no difference in CGT between the person who works 18-plus hours a day to create a business and the person who flicks through the TV channels while punting shares on their computer, I predict an even more enfeebled economy than we were anyway expecting.

On the subject of policymakers, who decided that people who have lived prudently, saved money and been financially responsible should now be penalised? I'm not saying we should expect life to be fair – anyone over the age of seven who says something "isn't fair" has a dismal grasp of reality – but it strikes me that those who have lived beyond their means are now being rewarded for having done so.

Next on my list of villains is British Airways. On a flight back from Dubai recently I was bumped from first into business class. They were very apologetic and gave me £500 (which I put straight into the company's bank account). But that was not the issue. I know that over-booking happens now and then, but in the lounge I encountered someone I knew. He was looking very smug. (He runs a PR company, so he probably looks smug all the time.) He had been upgraded to first class. What planet is Willie Walsh on, that he should let his airline upgrade someone in financial PR to first and – at a cost to his shareholders of £500 – downgrade me? It gets worse. At the gate, I met someone else I knew, also looking smug. He runs a political lobbying company and has a title. He had also been upgraded. Why was I moved down so that all these posturing flibbertigibbets – men, I might add – could scrape into first class?

Finally, my villains would have to include the FTSE-100 CEO who suggested I go on a diet, although he did redeem himself by sending me a bunch of beautiful flowers the day that I flew solo for the first time.

Heroes? My editor, Lionel Barber, for watching me fall base-over-apex down a marble flight of stairs and pretending that it never happened.

The Lovely Lucinda, for (among many other things) constantly repairing my battered bicycle, bought 10 years ago in Tokyo and still transporting me around central London. My girlfriends, not least my Artist Girlfriend, who originally suggested my

name to *FT Weekend* when they were looking for a columnist
in 1999. AG now lives in a large house in Oxford with no fewer
than two dishwashers, but still uses my column (and the *FT*
magazine) to stop the scrambled-egg saucepan marking the
table.

All the FTSE-100 CEOs who have shot on the line with me
and not suggested that I need to go on a diet. The editor of *The
Field*, Jonathan Young, for giving me an outlet to write about
shooting, so *FT Weekend* readers might be spared endless
accounts of the slaughter of innocent birds. And the flight
instructor who persevered with me until I was able to make that
solo flight – Richard White at Oxford Airport.

And finally, the man to whom I will have been married for 20
years on December 28. Happy anniversary, Mr M, who was
recently described by the England and Wales Cricket Board's
chairman as "the most maligned man in Britain". Maligned by
whom? It's all true, dear readers.

## THIS WILL BE THE YEAR OF LIVING CAREFULLY
*Jan 03, 2009*
So, welcome to 2009. What might the year have in store for
you? One thing's for sure: this recession will make it a testing
one for all of us, not least those who are still trying to deal with
the detritus of 2008.

One of my challenges this year is to recover money paid in
error into an account formerly held by our company at the
Icelandic bank Kaupthing Singer & Friedlander. Unfortunately,
this happened at the most inopportune moment possible – a few
days before the bank went into administration. Our attempts
to retrieve the money were unsuccessful, and so it was that
we discovered we were unsecured creditors of Kaupthing.
However, all is not lost. This is the age of the state bail-out
and we may be eligible for help under the Financial Services
Compensation Scheme, which was established to protect retail
deposits of £50,000 or less. As a small company we qualify for
the scheme, provided that we meet two of the following criteria:
turnover no higher than £6.5m; balance sheet total no more

than £3.26m; total staff of 50 or fewer. We qualify on all three
counts, and are owed a smidgen less than £50,000 so we have
filed a claim and will wait and see.

Another challenge will be to buy a birthday present for my
New Admirer. He took me out for dinner before Christmas and
presented me with a stunning gold bracelet. It turned out that he
had called the Lovely Lucinda to ask her what sort of jewellery
I like. She demurred, and passed him on to my Luxembourg
Employee, who is a natural stylist and chooses very good
jewellery. On being presented with the bracelet by NA, I put it
on my wrist. "Are you going to tell your husband?" he asked.
"Of course I am," I said. "How else am I going to explain it?
What would you say if your wife came home with this bracelet
on?" He thought about that for a moment. "She wouldn't," he
replied. "Why not?" "There is only one bracelet like that in the
world, the jeweller told me. How can she come home with it on
if you have it?"

Good point. So I shall be starting 2009 with a new bracelet. If
we don't get our money back from Kaupthing, I shall pawn it to
pay the school fees. What I shall not do is "regift" it. Not that I
am against regifting. In this economic climate, I am sure that I
shall be doing more and more of it. But I'm very keen indeed on
this bracelet, so I think I shall keep it for myself.

I usually give the women in my office Jo Malone body
products, but in these recessionary times I thought it appropriate
to be a little less extravagant. Instead, they all received body
products from the Body herself – Elle Macpherson, who is not
only a lingerie mogul, but also, I discovered, has a nifty line
in bath and body items. She tells me that Boots sells several
million pounds worth of these a year. Not in Wallingford, it
doesn't – I had to upgrade my Boots shopping to Oxford Street
and Piccadilly Circus to gather enough of them to go round. I
hope they will be enjoyed and not regifted.

On the other hand, I hope that the dozens of Jo Malone scented
candles languishing in the regifting cupboard at the office will
find new homes in 2009. Body cream (my body is not worth
putting cream on, even if I had time), perfume (I only wear one,

so any other goes straight into the cupboard) and other odds and ends will all be redirected. This is the year when I intend to clear out cupboards at home and at the office – we will all be so much less busy at work in 2009 that there will be plenty of time for this and other postponed pieces of housekeeping.

I am also going to write more letters. In this age of the internet and e-mail, a personal letter has so much more impact. My first letter of 2009 will be to all our clients to thank each of them for their continued support – even those who have paid our (very reasonable) fees into a collapsing Icelandic bank.

## WOULD ANYONE ELSE LIKE TO TELL ME I'M FAT?
*Jan 10, 2009*

G'Day. This is your Australian correspondent speaking. Usually by January 10 I will have graced a couple of shoots and attended the IFR Bank of the Year Awards, but 2009 is different. This year I have stayed on Down Under for a while to do some writing and teach a course at a university in Sydney.

Why have I turned my back on Britain for a few weeks? Surely it can't be the weather? No, I am fleeing the hordes of therapists that my colleagues and friends keep persuading me to try. In June last year, one of the women at work went to see a facial analyst in an attempt to lose weight. This was not just any facial analyst, it was the woman credited in the press with having helped Kate Winslet shed her post-baby pounds. My colleague promptly lost a stone, which encouraged many others to follow suit. Finally, with most of the office sending their outfits to Oxfam because they were too big, the Lovely Lucinda decided that I should see her too, and booked me in.

Even when surrounded by evidence that this was likely to work, I was deeply sceptical. Facial analysis is definitely rather alternative for me – right up there with organic vegetables and Pilates, I'm afraid. But I have already succumbed to Pilates, and so I went along. Her opening line to me – "My dear, you are a little dot of a thing. How did you put on so much weight?" – did little to put me at my ease. Neither was I soothed by the absence of makeup and nail varnish, a prerequisite of her consultations.

"If you lost some weight," she said, "you'd be quite pretty."
Amazingly I didn't walk out, and an hour later she sent me off
to buy a stack of supplements and gave me a list of what to eat
for the next fortnight. Every morning, for instance, I learnt that
I should eat porridge made with water, but without sugar or
anything else. This proved tricky, not least because I had to go
to Hong Kong and Dubai that week and, rather oddly, porridge
seemed in short supply. I also eschewed tea, coffee and alcohol,
which was easier than I thought, although giving up coffee
proved a revelation. I didn't have headaches from caffeine
withdrawal, but I did discover how much of a social prop coffee
was for me, like cigarettes for smokers. I found myself sitting in
Starbucks feeling a total fraud, while everyone around me dosed
up on caffeine and I drank poncey caffeine-free tea.

I'm not sure that I'm an especially good candidate for
facial analysis, or at least not for the strict regime required
to achieve weight loss. My trainer, Holly the Sadist, was
encouraged to learn that I was trying to eat more healthily. She
suggested another way to make me feel better and fitter – a
sports massage. Why oh why did I agree to this? I am far too
biddable. "Tell me," said the masseur, "why did you book an
appointment?" "Because HTS suggested it," I said. "After she
got me to try colonic irrigation last year, sports massage sounds
like a walk in the park."

It wasn't. It hurt like hell. If I had known what it would be like
I'd have asked for an epidural before we started. My muscles
were as tight as a drum but after a great deal of painful work my
flexibility improved no end. Darcey Bussell I may not be, but if
it wasn't for the pain I would highly recommend the massage.
"You'd be even more flexible," the masseur informed me, "if
you weren't quite so well-padded."

I promise you, I'm really not that fat. I can still get into
clothes sold in normal shops. I have not had to have my bed
strengthened. I could probably do with losing a few (well,
more than a few) pounds and I certainly need to do more
exercise. Which is why I am not eating and drinking my way
through January at shoots and banking awards dinners, and

why I remain in Australia, as far away as I can get from facial analysis. And sports massage.

## WE MUST DIG DEEP IN SEARCH OF REASONS TO SMILE
*Jan 31, 2009*

Snow, snappers and sandwiches. The World Economic Forum at Davos always has its share of snow and plenty of photographers looking for that outstanding picture of a leading business figure or politician standing in it. But the food at Davos is usually rather grander than sandwiches. This year, however, the gathering is likely to have a very different mood to 2008.

This time last year, a hot topic for debate was the looming presence of sovereign wealth funds. Most people had never heard of them until late 2007 when they started putting capital into banks that were looking wobbly. Wobbly banks loomed large too, mainly thanks to an announcement from Société Générale on the Wednesday of the 2008 meeting that a rogue trader had cost it a lot of money. But there was no shortage of parties, and certainly no need to spend any money on feeding myself.

This year we will all be much more sombre. Banks that have received large quantities of taxpayers' money will not be able to justify spending it on lavish meals for assorted luminaries and journalists. I suspect we will all be eating much more humble fare, and may even have to pay for it ourselves.

The recession is affecting us all, and in many more ways than just limiting how many canapés I will be offered in Davos. People are losing their jobs, their homes and in some tragic cases, their lives. Writing a column that is supposed to entertain is challenging in the face of the biggest recession in our lifetime. Even if the economic problems are self-inflicted, the human toll that they will take this year and next will leave very little to smile about, in Davos or in Doncaster.

But I am an optimist, even in these difficult times. And just as the delegates in Davos will be trying to establish how they can work together to revive the world economy, it will be the friends we have made, and what we have been prepared to do for them, that will define the winners and losers over the next year or so. As I said to a graduating university class the other day, the phrase "I can't do it" should not be in their vocabulary. Instead, it should be "I can't do it alone."

I try to support my friends whenever I can. Their requests are sometimes small and sometimes large. While in Australia recently, I agreed to spend part of a precious free morning getting a house ready for a viewing by a prospective buyer. While in the kitchen, I answered a call from my New Admirer in the UK where it was the end of the day. Without an earpiece, I cradled the phone between neck and ear so that I could use both hands at the sink and continue to speak. All went well until I finished the washing up and took out several empty milk cartons and wine bottles to the recycling bin. Australia is big on recycling and each household has a substantial wheelie bin for this purpose.

Leaning over the bin (which was almost as tall as me) I suddenly felt the phone slip away and, before I could stop it, it was at the bottom of the bin. I leaned in, but it was far too tall for me to reach more than halfway down. Anyone walking to the beach in Victor Harbor that day would have seen a middle-aged woman screaming into a recycling bin, "don't worry, NA, hang in there, I will rescue you in just a minute" – as if a real person of Lilliputian proportions had fallen in and was awaiting rescue. It is a measure of NA's patience and enthusiasm to speak to me that, after I had upended the bin and sorted through pizza packaging and assorted beer bottles to retrieve my telephone, he was still there. "What happened?" he asked. "I just recycled you," I explained.

Recycling admirers (I have many girlfriends to look after) is an admirable idea, especially as I am married. Plus I was grateful for something to smile about. Smiles, unlike sandwiches, might be scarce in the snow this year.

CHANGE WE CAN BELIEVE IN – INCLUDING HOCKEY
*Feb 07, 2009*
The US voted for change, and now at last it has come. Unlike

the UK, where we vote one day and a new prime minister moves into 10 Downing Street the next, the incoming administration in Washington DC has a couple of months to prepare for government. This might be frustrating for them (and for the people who voted for change) but I suspect that the work of the transition team improves the chances of effective government from day one.

I was in Melbourne for the inauguration, which required a 3am alarm call so that I could watch it live. I am not a US citizen, but along with millions of others around the world I felt I was participating in a unique historical event.

Of course the last time the US elected a president on the Democratic ticket, who was also in his forties and born in August, we ended up with the repeal of the Glass-Steagall Act (a 60-year-old cornerstone of US banking regulation) and the direction to US lenders to offer mortgages to people who, it turned out, were unlikely to be able to repay them. And look where that has got us. But I don't want to rain on the Obama parade and I have been encouraged by the response of young people to the idea of change in the US via the ballot box. Back in November, on the day of the US election, I received another alarm call, this time from Cost Centre #1, who was in a different time zone to me and, at the age of 19, was overcome with emotion at the election of a president he had never met to the leadership of a country of which he was not a citizen, or even resident in, via a ballot that he had not participated in.

Both he and CC#2, one in Sydney, the other in Crowthorne, watched the inauguration live. CC#2 is just as enthusiastic. He has also embraced change, in his case by taking up hockey. He returned to school in January in freezing temperatures to discover that he needed a hockey stick and did not have the written permission he required in order to use my credit card. With his parents still in Australia and fast asleep, and the Lovely Lucinda on holiday in Thailand, it fell to my colleague and Most Tenacious Girlfriend to take his call in the office and make the purchase. I had left MTG with my power of attorney while away, but had not anticipated that it would cover the purchase of hockey sticks.

After I thanked her by e-mail the next day, she responded: "Even if the recession gets so bad that you have to withdraw CC#2 from school due to lack of funds I don't think it would make an iota of difference. His utter charm and manners will get him a long way and if he has the capacity to talk to a complete stranger as comfortably as he talked to me, he'll be fine. He even dealt with the question 'are you sure I'm not handing my credit card over for you to enjoy porn, drugs or alcohol?' very well – the chirpy little response was 'it wouldn't be sensible to use a credit card for any of those'!"

An even bigger change when CC#2 started at this school back in September, at the age of 13, was his adoption of e-mail, which he rarely bothered with in prep school. Lacking a transition team to prepare him, he was overwhelmed by mails and by Christmas had more than 200 in his inbox unread, including some from his parents. An endless stream of all-school e-mails was to blame, from announcements of the arrival of Krispy Kreme donuts in the tuck shop, to a plea from someone who has mislaid their chemistry file, to changes of time for chapel and so on.

His reaction has been to read anything from the teachers and ignore the rest. Thank goodness for the new leader of the free world. Without electronic media, I have explained to CC#2, he would never have been elected. We have the first black president, but we also have the first BlackBerry-carrying one. As CC#2 is discovering for himself, managing one's e-mail is a vital skill in the process of change.

A FEW HIGHS – BUT A LOT OF MOUNTAINS STILL TO CLIMB...
*Feb 14, 2009*
Happy Valentine's Day David Rubenstein – you summed up Davos for me. The co-founder of Carlyle, a large American private equity group, said that while he had heard plenty of theories during the World Economic Forum annual meeting about why the world was in this economic and financial mess, he'd heard almost none suggesting how to go about fixing it.

The sombre mood at Davos was tempered, however, by the pleasure of seeing some of the people whose company I really enjoy. One of these was Sarah Brown, whose personal advocacy for the fifth Millennium Development Goal – the reduction of maternal mortality – was evident in her speech at the Important Dinner for Women given by Wendi Murdoch and Indra Nooyi, CEO of PepsiCo. On this occasion, at least, we were not only told what the problem was – 500,000 women die in childbirth each year, and no progress has been made in reducing this since the goals were laid down in 2000 – but we were each given a card setting out six suggestions of how to help, and were asked by Elisabeth Murdoch to commit to at least one of them:

1. Visit to a key Millennium Development Goal country to see what needs to be done;
2. Ask for a meeting with a key politician on the issue;
3. Set up an initiative at work to encourage your colleagues to do something to help;
4. Use Mother's Day to communicate how we can improve the health of mothers around the world and the importance of mothers to the future prosperity of us all;
5. Contribute financially to the campaign;
6. Develop your own idea of how you can make a difference on this crucial subject.

A problem and some suggested solutions. Mr Rubenstein would have approved, but of course he was not at the dinner, as it was for women only – although Rupert Murdoch did appear at the end to help us with our coats.

My other Valentine's pin-ups are the four speakers at the Credit Suisse lunch I attended. Duncan Niederauer of the New York Stock Exchange, who pointed out that (unlike some other exchanges) his had stayed open every day throughout the crisis last September, and that he was sick of being asked by the media if it was going to close. The other three were Steve Schwarzman from Blackstone (forthright as ever); Jes Staley from JP Morgan; and the star of the show, Eric Mindich of Eton Park Capital Management, once Goldman Sachs' youngest ever partner.

So, plenty of gloom at Davos, but here are 10 of the less serious revelations from the snow this year:

1. Adair Turner, chair of the Financial Services Authority and the government's climate change tsar, can dance;
2. Robin Buchanan, the president of London Business School, can ski – but not as well as Reuters' Tom Glocer and his wife, Maarit;
3. Tammy Haddad from Newsweek and I make a formidable team. Yes, Richard Branson, that's how you came to be interviewed on TamCam;
4. HRH the Duke of York had the most impressively shined shoes at the WEF;
5. Being photographed with Sarah Brown, Wendi Murdoch and Naomi Campbell is not a good idea if you already have self-esteem issues;
6. Anshu Jain, the head of Deutsche Bank's global markets division, lives up to his billing. And his wife is incredibly attractive;
7. Friede Springer, the widow of German media tycoon Axel Springer and deputy chair of his newspaper company, is very good company and uncommonly knowledgeable about Finland;
8. The shuttle from Klosters to Davos is a great place to meet people;
9. Swiss trains are cheap, efficient and even used by Kofi Annan;
10. Next year I want to meet David Rubenstein.

## IF YOU CARE ABOUT POPULARITY, DON'T RUN A BUSINESS
*Feb 21, 2009*
What is the hardest professional decision you have ever made? Mine is the one that I was forced to take at the start of this year. Twelve thousand miles away in Australia, with time to think and plan for my business, I realised that although I had put in place many precautions against an economic downturn, they were not enough in the face of the worst recession in many, many years. People account for 80 per cent of the costs in our business. So, if you need to cut costs, you have to cut people. I can cancel my

shooting, give up our garage lease, travel second class, catch the tube and so on, but this is all fiddling around at the edges. I had warned the team months ago that bonuses in 2009 were out, as were pay rises for anyone earning more than £30,000. But this, too, was not enough. Real, substantial cost-cutting means saying goodbye to people.

The bizarre part of all this is that we are as busy as ever. But fees are under pressure, as any service-industry boss will tell you, and competition is fierce. We are good at what we do and have an enviable reputation, supported by a 26-year track record. But that is not enough to insulate us completely from the winds of change that are blowing through the world economy this year – and probably next. We are profitable and cash-positive, and I want to stay that way. Which we won't if I do nothing but sit on my hands and hope that everything will somehow get better.

I learned long ago that running a business – just like parenting – is not a popularity contest. If you are the sort of person who needs constant thanks and adulation, don't try either of these activities. You get none of the praise when things go right and all of the blame when they go wrong. So I knew I couldn't delegate this – I would have to make the hard decisions, and take the emotional fallout myself.

I am not a believer in voluntary redundancy. You will inevitably lose the people who can most easily get another job – your top performers. Neither am I in favour of unilateral wage cuts to preserve jobs.

You will end up with people sitting around being resentful of each other. So, in our case, we have had a round of compulsory redundancies and negotiated voluntary pay cuts with those who remain, to get us into the kind of shape in which I think we need to be when facing unprecedented – at least in my lifetime – market conditions.

It helps to be 12,000 miles away from home when you have to think the hitherto unthinkable. You can get over the sleepless nights and through the boxes of tissues that, if you have any heart, you will need, and your employees won't see the bags under your tear-stained eyes. "If you don't bleed emotionally when you do this, then you are not human – that's what I tell my managers," said one of the FTSE 100 chief executives with whom I shared all this.

Well, by the time I returned to the UK I had survived the rapids of emotional turmoil and entered a calm sea of objectivity. I discussed my plan with my senior team, and took their advice. And it helped that, halfway through my thought processes, I learned that I too had been sacked. The editor of *The Field* e-mailed me to let me know that, after a 15-month stint as a columnist, he would not be requiring my services any more. The March issue, for which I had already filed, would be my last. No boxes of tissues for him, I am sure. And he didn't even do me the courtesy of pretending it was because he needed to cut costs. No, I was too controversial. Me?

Well, the Lovely Lucinda is not too controversial. But sadly she is not essential either. I can no longer justify the luxury of having a PA when I am making cuts elsewhere. So, back to rescuing my own BlackBerry from cabs and running my own diary. I did it once and I am sure I will manage it again. But it didn't make the decision any easier.

## RAGE AGAINST THE COFFEE MACHINE
*Feb 28, 2009*

It's quite possible that education is a complete waste of time. That was my conclusion, having tangled with a coffee machine in Switzerland recently. I had escaped, courtesy of a very cheap ticket, to the Alps to redo the cashflow forecasts for my business in preparation for a visit to the (still solvent) bank. A generous friend lent me his beautiful chalet, complete with Sky TV (which enabled me to listen to Radio 4), an 18m swimming pool and a coffee machine.

It was a Nespresso machine, and we have one at work, so you would have thought that I could have coped. But (a) ours is a bit more basic and (b) I have never used it. I struggle to get enthusiastic about "proper" coffee - instant works fine for me - and I am always suspicious about anything that feels the need to employ George Clooney in its advertising.

Now, I am sure that Mr Clooney is a thoroughly engaging individual with a sparkling line in dinner conversation and is, no doubt, a coffee connoisseur to boot. My Pilates-Loving Girlfriend says he is the only man she has ever met who is as attractive in the flesh as on screen. (PLG, you need to meet Anshu Jain, head of global markets at Deutsche Bank). Be that as it may, we acquired an office Nespresso machine because my colleagues were fed up with instant and, as regular readers know, I cannot operate a coffee plunger.

After two days at the chalet, I (with my three academic degrees) had worked out how to insert the coffee capsules into the machine, but not how to stop it from squashing them, as opposed to extracting their contents. Also, the machine seemed to be out of water and I could not figure out how to switch on the thing. A further day and some careful consultation with the caretaker (one degree, in planning) led us to a power switch at the back of the machine. We also realised that we needed to remove the reservoir on the front and fill it with water. However, the machine continued to squash the capsules, and the water didn't pump through.

One more day elapsed before the arrival of my Longest Standing Girlfriend (degree in engineering, postgraduate degree in marketing and an MBA). She solved the problem of the squashed capsules (one has to open the lid all the way, which ejects the previous capsule) but not the problem of the water. Just then, our absent and gorgeous host (who is even better-looking than George Clooney) e-mailed me to see if all was well. I replied that the only concern was the coffee machine. He explained our problem - the reservoir at the front was for milk! The water reservoir was in a concealed drawer at the bottom.

Can education really affect the quality of what we put into our mouths? After all, we had seven degrees between the three of us yet were unable to ensure that we were drinking decent coffee. It seemed a relevant question this week, after I learned that a school in the UK has offered a sixth-form scholarship to any student prepared to turn vegetarian; the school had been founded with vegetarian principles (and, very probably, a vegetarian principal).

Then I discovered that the mother of one of my godchildren, not yet three and with a healthy dislike of vegetables, is sending him to vegetable classes. Vegetable classes? Yes, you can send your toddler to vegetable classes; if you live in south London, you needn't stop at Tumble Tots or music. Where were vegetable classes when Cost Centre #1 was growing up with the notion that chips are vegetables? As my godson's aunt pointed out, we all had vegetable classes delivered by our parents - the syllabus was very short: "You are not getting down from the table until you have eaten what is on your plate."

Vegetable classes cost £110 a term and the three-year-old in question is still not eating vegetables. I suspect education isn't going to make the slightest difference in his case, either.

### IN LOVE AND IN LOSS, ACTIONS SPEAK LOUDER THAN WORDS
*Mar 07, 2009*

Sometimes words are not enough. I used plenty of them five years ago when my Single Girlfriend showed signs of becoming attached to her personal trainer. Madonna may have had a baby with hers, but that doesn't mean the rest of us should. In the end, I decided that acta non verba was the motto of the day, and started taking her with me to meet as many single men as possible.

I started, on February 9 2004, by taking her to a party thrown by my friend the Eligible Banker. Eligible because not married, not gay and solvent. The party was to celebrate his management buyout and, though he shook SG's hand, no words were exchanged. I resorted to fixing a double dinner date with SG, me, EB and a former client of his.

This time words were exchanged. SG and EB talked well into the night. But then it looked for a while as if words were all that their relationship would amount to. They met for coffee a few times and even went to the cinema, but nothing happened. "What's wrong with you?" I demanded of SG. "Just jump on him! Acta non verba!" I threatened to sign her up to an internet dating site if he stopped seeing her.

I invited them both to join me at a function at the Grosvenor House hotel. SG scrubbed up and EB looked gorgeous in black tie, as most men do. When EB left, SG saw him out. She returned some time later. Why did you bother? I demanded. Her reply showed me that EB had finally abandoned talking for action. "I didn't want to stop snogging him," she replied.

One of the reasons I was convinced that they would get on well was that they were both chartered accountants. He had qualified with Touche Ross in Leeds, she with KPMG in Sydney. This proved both the glue and the friction in their relationship. Neither could agree who was the senior partner. Long after they had fallen in love, had a baby and bought a house, they were still in dispute about which bathroom tiles to buy for their ensuite. "What's wrong with you?" I asked SG, again. "Don't you know better than to give any man a say over something like bathroom tiles? Stop discussing it with him and order the tiles! Acta non verba!"

They moved in together in spring 2005. Or rather, she moved in with him. I helped her move. Until then, I had never stopped to consider just how much stuff a bachelor can amass if he remains unmarried into his late thirties. There was nowhere for SG's kitchen equipment, her shoe collection looked destined for a bin liner and as for anywhere to put her cosmetics ... "What's wrong with you?" I asked. "Just chuck all his stuff out!" But she demurred, and somehow it all fitted in.

One more baby and even in a new house space was at a premium. EB was particularly resistant to the idea of flogging his spherical bookcase on eBay. So SG again forged a compromise and it now sits in the children's room with clothes, books and toys on it, testament to who really was the senior partner.

EB called me the other day and after talking shop for a few minutes he asked me to drop in and see SG. He was going to South Africa for a week on business, and he thought she might be lonely. SG herself called me three days later. But her words were overwhelmed by tears. And when I made it back from my business trip the next day to be by her side, we didn't use words at all. We just held each other and cried.

EB had collapsed and died while out walking on Table Mountain, one day short of the fifth anniversary of the first time they met. EB, wherever you are, I have called in several times. Right now, when I see SG and your two beautiful boys, I don't have the right words. But I promise I will try to show them over the years to come how much you all mean to me. Acta non verba.

## SURVIVAL OF THE FITTEST IS GREAT, ESPECIALLY IF YOU'RE THE FITTEST
*Mar 14, 2009*

Darwin would have approved. The writing looks to be on the wall for many of the UK's private schools, and my prediction is that only the fittest will survive. Many families, ours included, are looking at how they educate their children and considering something that hitherto would have been blasphemy in many a middle-class British household – private education, it turns out, may be a discretionary expense after all.

Therefore, demand for private education will decline, and some schools will not survive. Is this a bad thing? I like the idea that only the fittest survive. And when an organisation goes out of business, the consequences may not always be bad for those associated with it.

My former school has just announced that it is shutting its doors this summer. (Those of you who groan every week at my excessive liking for adjectives and substandard application of grammar might consider this welcome news.) Established in 1846 to educate the daughters of clergy, it had extended its remit to the secular world long before I arrived in 1974. It was a perfectly OK school in its way, but I have not been back since I left and am not shedding tears over its demise. The things I took away from my school – some excellent teaching, notably in Latin, maths and economics (not English, note) – and some lifelong friends, will always be with me. I am not concerned about the bricks and mortar.

So I am not feeling sentimental about its closure, and in one way I am even delighted (not overwhelmingly delighted, note, or totally delighted, or even surprisingly delighted). Not only is it closing, it is being absorbed into the nearest girls' school, which happens to be Roedean. What a result! I always wanted to go to Roedean, but it was far too posh for my family and was never considered. Now it seems I can claim to have attended it posthumously. The closest I ever came to Roedean while of school age was our annual lacrosse fixture there. We had to walk to the match (it was less than a mile), past the Brighton College playing fields, and then fight it out against a much better team on their windswept pitch, often in the pouring rain. I have since chosen to keep the association going vicariously by employing someone who attended Roedean. But I never dreamed it would absorb my old school.

So the net effect of one organisation going out of business is to considerably (or substantially or even flatteringly) enhance my CV. And why stop at consolidation in education? Consolidation elsewhere can be just as advantageous. I used to work for a British stockbroker that was bought by a Dutch bank that was in turn bought by a Scottish bank. I will, therefore, one day be an RBS pensioner, although sadly (extremely sadly), my entitlement stands at nowhere near the £16m accumulated by Sir Fred Goodwin. I confess that I was concerned (even slightly concerned, or very concerned) as RBS took on more and more debt, that it might go bust and not be able to pay me when the time comes. But look at what has happened now – RBS is owned by Her Majesty's Government. I suppose it is possible (even entirely possible) that HMG will run out of money and will not be able to pay me, but I must say that I watched RBS slide into public ownership with a great sense of relief. I now have a government-backed pension, something that many people in the UK will surely covet.

An upgraded CV and an upgraded pension. And the party is not over yet. This recession has a long way to go, but so far it seems to have paid dividends. Which is more than many businesses will be able to do this year. Which in turn will have an effect on people's income. And their ability to pay school fees. Which will encourage more consolidation. The fittest will survive – and that's a very good thing. (Or even a fabulously good thing. Or an amazingly good thing. Or … )

## If only you managed to keep mum, Mr M
*Mar 21, 2009*

How important is your mother to you? No, this is not the question that I pose to the Cost Centres, who I swear think that mothers are just a cross between a taxi service and a cashpoint. It is a question that I dwell on at this time of the year, because tomorrow is the fourth Sunday in Lent, and in the UK we celebrate Mothering Sunday.

Originally a day when people returned to their "mother" church, it has become a calendar date similar to the maternal celebrations held in the US and Australia (and elsewhere) every May. Which means that if you are a US or Australian citizen living in the UK (and we have many of them, Mr M included), you have to remember to buy a card this week and then keep it in a drawer until May before posting it. This should not be beyond the wit of men, but frequently is.

For Mother's Day this year I was going to buy my mother James McIntosh's *Mix*, which recently won the 2008 Gourmand award for the UK's best cookbook series and in these days of austerity retails for a mere £4.99. But I decided it looked a bit mean (not only is the book cheap, it is also very small) and so instead I got McIntosh himself to come and demonstrate recipes from it on my Aga for my mother and me. That then seemed a bit extravagant (it's hard to get these things right), so I invited half a dozen other friends to come along as well. We sat in my kitchen on hard-backed chairs, watching him turn out everything from a fried egg to homemade bread, and learning how to make perfect sponge cakes. It was like having a magician at a children's birthday party, except better, because we got to eat the results.

Mr M did not attend. He had been playing golf in the morning and then took himself off to watch a school sports fixture in the afternoon. Standing around watching Northern Ireland's

30-year-old answer to Martha Stewart cooking for an audience on our Aga evidently did not figure on his list of ideal ways to spend a Saturday afternoon. But he was interested in what I would be cooking for dinner.

This was because we were taking part in the village "safari supper", during which people volunteer to host one course of a dinner in their home, and are allocated guests randomly. Or not so randomly, it transpires; I was told by the organiser that when invited to send in their dietary requirements, some people in our village also sent in their fellow-guest requirements.

So, six complete strangers were coming to our house for their first course. We would then go on to a main course with another six and dessert with six more. Altogether, I would sit down to eat with 18 different people that evening, in three different houses, of which one was my own. "What are we serving for our starter?" asked Mr M, when he finally returned home at 4pm. "Butternut squash soup," I replied. "Couldn't you have done better than that?" he asked.

At this, I didn't just hit the roof, I went right through it and into orbit around Pluto. How dare he swan off to play golf at 8.30am, barely reappear at lunch and then disappear again all afternoon to stand on a hockey touchline, only returning to criticise my selection of starter? If he wanted something more sophisticated, why had he not stayed home to cook it? It turned out that he thought I had engaged McIntosh to prepare the starter, and so he was expecting something fancier than butternut squash soup.

Well, as it happens, I had got McIntosh to prepare the starter, although I chose it. He has not yet written a book on starters (his second book, *Dinner*, consists of main courses only). And I served his homemade bread, which I loved. And so did our guests. And so did my mother. So there, Mr M. And by the way, you have six weeks to get ready for your own Mother's Day.

No MINISTER, IT IS NOT SMART TO GIVE BONUSES A BAD NAME
*Mar 28, 2009*
Bonus is a Latin word. It means good. Nowadays it is used over and over again by people who have never studied Latin

and probably regard it as a dead language taught to toffs. As usual, abuse of language and over-reaction leave us in the UK in danger of throwing out a perfectly good management tool simply because it has become synonymous with excessive greed.

The last time this happened, the private equity industry was almost single-handedly responsible for landing us with a flat, 18 per cent rate of capital gains tax. This made no distinction between the tax levied on entrepreneurs such as me, who put in sweat equity and risk finance to create jobs and build businesses, and people who punt stocks and shares from their living room without making any meaningful contribution to the economy. Now it is going to happen again.

The government here plans to use its ownership of high-street banks to enforce changes in the way their staff are compensated. But as usual, the politicians have adopted a one-size-fits-all approach and so the sins of the few will be paid for by the many.

I have long believed that the real threat to London's position as a global financial centre is not its exorbitant commercial rents, nor the ludicrous cost of a gin and tonic at The Berkeley hotel (£11), but the nature of the press coverage it attracts. The banking crisis here has seen the media (with obvious honourable exceptions) descend into near-hysteria over anything called a "bonus", assuming that, by definition, it must be an unearned, undeserved perk.

Now, we all know people who have earned far too much for far too long, doing far too little. I am not here to defend the sums paid to many stockbrokers, investment bankers and hedge fund managers over the past decade or so. But I object to the way that the public outcry over a relatively small number of bonus payments has been manipulated. This has allowed government ministers and remuneration committees to affect the lives of hundreds of thousands of people for whom an annual bonus has been exactly that – a treat, something good. For most people, the sums involved do not run into tens of thousands of pounds, let alone millions.

Incentive pay is an excellent management tool. If you are trying to encourage the people who work behind the counter in banks to reduce queuing time, increase cross-selling of products and improve customer satisfaction, paying them a few hundred pounds extra at the end of the year if they achieve that is a smart thing to do. Not only does it incentivise them (and how else are you going to change behaviour?), it keeps down fixed costs. Bonuses are not usually pensionable, and if you have to lay off staff, their redundancy costs will be based only on their salaries. It makes total sense to allow people to earn additional amounts if they deliver against worthwhile targets.

Should bonuses be linked to longer-term performance? Probably, but not solely. Changes in behaviour need to be immediate – who will change their behaviour if it results in a small amount of money in the distant future?

I would prefer the government to stay away from compensation arrangements. I would prefer the press to understand what a bonus really is. In our business, if we make more than our threshold profit, we distribute it to the employees. Some of this is delayed for three years and is subject to the continuing financial health of the company. I suspect we will not be making any such payments this year, but I hope very much that we will do so again before long.

And I am going to rename them. I have been considering lucrum (as in lucrums will be payable again once the economy improves). Any suggestions? Anything is better than having the government hijack our compensation, our share registers and now even our language.

## ECHOES OF JAPAN'S LOST DECADE ON A SCOTTISH HILLSIDE
*Apr 04, 2009*

Mum, what's the "carry trade"? Cost Centre #2, he of the challenging questions, posed this one halfway up a hill in Scotland during our last break together. It took me a while to get my breath back (he marches uphill much faster than I do) so I had time to frame an answer in terms suitable for a 14-year-old who reads the *FT Weekend Magazine* and so was familiar

with the cover story that weekend on Japanese housewives.
I used to be a Japanese housewife of sorts, although, in truth, I
wasn't Japanese and wasn't a housewife. But the Moneypenny
family lived in Tokyo from 1998 until 2000 and so were in
Japan at the end of the "lost decade", or *ushinawareta junen*. It
was there, 10 years ago, that I started writing this column.
Years later, I published the Japanese columns in a collection
entitled *E-mail from Tokyo*. Reading through it now makes
me realise anew how it feels to have no economic growth and
interest rates effectively at zero, as we do now. The Japanese
were then inching their way back to success, very carefully.
Credit was difficult to come by, the banks had been bailed
out by the government and frugality was the order of the day
- exactly as I imagine things are going to be here in Britain for
a very long time. Unemployment was a way of life, other than
for the highly skilled, and there were rigorous immigration
controls. So much so that Mr M's visa application was met with
resistance as the Japanese authorities questioned why someone
who had not completed any higher education should be allowed
to come and work there. (Mr M suggested that they should
average out our combined university degrees, which would
have given him 1.5.) In spite of all this, I loved living in Japan
and learnt a lot about Japanese culture, which I wrote about for
*FT* readers each week.

The column was interspersed with comments about my
children, then young (one, five and nine when I started) and
not yet labelled Cost Centres. There was a lot of debate in
Britain last month about whether parents who write for public
consumption should do so about their offspring. This was in
response to Julie Myerson's book, *The Lost Child*, in which she
describes her experience of evicting her son from the family
home because of his drug use. I have never evicted any of the
Cost Centres for any reason at all but I have written about them
for public consumption. Myerson says that she showed her son
her book to get his approval before publishing it. Why? I have
never done anything so touchy-feely and liberal. My family
show no hesitation in spending the money that I earn, from

writing or indeed anything else, so it would be hypocritical of them to complain about the way I earn it.

CC#2 and I chatted happily about many things during our time in Scotland, including the value of higher education, single-sex schools and profit margins on mobile phone contracts. After all this, one evening he turned to me and said in a very matter-of-fact voice: "Mum, it is good chatting to you. It's nice to have someone to talk to about topics other than sex and the size of my dick." I am clearly behind the curve on teenage boys.

Cost Centre #1 is away on his gap year in Australia and so, other than the occasional telephone call, I can't talk to him about anything, not even sex or how well endowed he is. He has a second credit card on my account, which is intended to extend my travel insurance to him and to take care of emergencies. Looking at my statement last month, it became clear that his definition of an emergency was some way from my own. Accessing credit in one currency in order to acquire assets in another (albeit via an off-licence) is, I explained to his younger brother, a very good illustration of what the carry trade is all about.

## HOW DID I CELEBRATE MY BIRTHDAY? I GOT OUT MY GUN
*Apr 11, 2009*

Happy Easter. Here in the UK we have two bank holidays in celebration of Christ's death and resurrection, which will make for an extra-long weekend. The evenings are lighter, since we moved to British Summer Time on March 29, and I am heavier, having eaten and drunk to celebrate my 47th birthday on March 27. So a weekend of exercise is called for.

Forty-seven is not a particularly important milestone, but I do like celebrating birthdays and in particular my own. It is a tradition in my office that on, or near, the date we invite about 70 women to spend the day clay pigeon shooting with us, and this year we held the event in deepest Berkshire, at the establishment run by Dylan Williams. Williams is a perfectionist – clean and tidy desk, clean and tidy shooting school, smartly presented instructors. I have attended several clay shooting days organised by Williams and his team, some simulated game shoots and even some real ones. They all run like clockwork and an almost unbelievable amount of work goes in beforehand to prepare. It will not surprise you to learn that I am a much more spontaneous sort of person. I wouldn't last five minutes working for Williams, and I don't improve with age. I am just as bad at 47 as I was at 46.

So, while I was very grateful that our day in Berkshire was well organised and timed to perfection, I was very amused when even Williams was wrong-footed. The arrival of 70 women at his establishment, many of whom had never held a gun before, presented him with an organisational challenge that even he had not foreseen. We all congregated for breakfast and then went out in groups for tuition. At this point, the room we had been occupying was reconfigured for our mid-morning coffee break. At least, that was the plan. In practice, before any furniture could be rearranged, the Williams team had to decide what to do with 70 handbags.

It is very interesting to see the types of handbag that 70 over-achieving women bring with them for a day of clay pigeon shooting. It is also very interesting to see how they get on when wielding a gun rather than a BlackBerry. One previous participant told me that she owed her success to a simple trick – she pretended that every clay pigeon was her ex-husband. Personally, I pretend that every clay pigeon is an administrator of Kaupthing Singer & Friedlander, since despite repeated requests for a meeting with them, I have been denied one. Perhaps I should try going round there with a gun.

The winners of both our novice and "more experienced shot" competitions are happily married, and not in dispute with a failed Icelandic bank, so they can't have been using either of those tactics. But the best shot of all, whom we had disqualified from the individual competition, was Abbey Burton, who, at 22, was the youngest woman there by more than 10 years. We are a tiny business but even we like to feel that we are participating in some way in London 2012, and so we sponsor Burton, who is in the Great Britain shooting team for Olympic Trap. She has won European and world silver medals, and we all hope she will qualify.

Burton has only been shooting for six years and like many dedicated aspirant Olympians devotes every waking hour to practice and competition, or to earning the money to practise and compete. We agreed to start sponsoring her a year ago, sight unseen, and so we were delighted finally to meet her. And after watching Burton shoot, no one was bothered about what kind of handbag she was carrying.

So, this weekend I shall be flying, shooting and picking up my training schedule to make up for all those extra glasses of wine and white chocolate treats. Which, of course, are what my family produce for me on my birthday and at Easter. Next year, please, another handbag!

### IN A LATHER ABOUT EQUAL OPPORTUNITY SPIN CYCLES
*Apr 25, 2009*

Do you share a house or a flat with someone? I have lived communally all my life. I grew up in a boarding school, and out of term-time lived with my family; I abandoned halls of residence for a flat after only a term; I shared flats and mortgages with girlfriends until I was married; and for the last 20 years I have shared a home with Mr M and the Cost Centres. I think that sharing a house with someone for 20 years merits a medal. Other people's habits can drive me insane (and I am sure mine do in return). Lavatory seats, for instance: a house full of boys tends to mean that they are always left up. I prefer them to be left down. Other people would prefer that not only seats but also lids be left down, too.

We could go on. Laundry is an area that raises strong emotions. I will do the family's laundry and fold it up, but I do draw the line at putting it away. I will not raise an equal opportunity household if I wait on them all, hand and foot. Nor will their future wives thank me (and that includes any future wife of Mr M). But Mr M appears perfectly happy to live with piles of clean laundry sitting around the room and doesn't mind that the clothes never find their way into a drawer or on to a hanger.

If laundry etiquette is a charged issue at home, it is even more fraught at work. We encourage our team to cycle to work and so provide bathrooms for them to use on arrival. We also have a laundry for the washing of all our towels and tea towels and any personal items that staff might wish to wash. Since many of them get changed into their work clothes at the office, some wash their work shirts in the communal laundry.

As do I. I recently went to wash some clothes (that I needed clean for the next day) just before leaving for a dinner engagement. To my disgust, I found the washing machine full of shirts, and no laundry detergent at all. Just an empty box. I didn't mind having to move the shirts into the drier but I could not understand why the perpetrator had failed to alert anyone to the absence of detergent. Surely it is a bad career move to leave your boss high and dry when she comes to wash her shirt at 6.30pm?

Fortunately, I knew that the Lovely Lucinda was at a job interview four doors down. I sent her an emergency text, so she went to the shop afterwards and returned to the office to start the machine.

LL has gone now, a victim of the economic slowdown which has affected almost everyone, us included. How am I coping without her? Badly. Which is exactly as the latest issue of *Executary News*, "the news magazine for executive secretaries and PAs" (so perhaps less than wholly impartial in this matter), predicted in a back-page item which lambasted me for thinking I could do without her.

Argument is divided as to whether a PA is a luxury or a necessity, but – rightly or wrongly – I felt it was appropriate that I try to manage without her. Fortunately, she has accepted the job offer four doors down and will be on hand for emergencies. Such as detergent.

At work, not only do I move laundry to the drier but I empty that, too, and fold everything up, regardless of whose it is or what it contains. My male colleagues are less considerate and just dump my stuff out of the drier into a heap in my room. We have had a heated debate about why they don't sort it out, fold it up, match socks, etc, as I do for them. They argue that while my action in sorting out their underwear is motherly, their reciprocating could be construed as perversion. I could just dump theirs, too, I suppose, but I am genetically modified to sort and fold laundry. And report detergent shortages. And live communally. With or without the Lovely Lucinda.

## WHY WOMEN DESERVE TO REAP THE AWARDS
*May 09, 2009*

I have never won an award. This may well be because there are no awards in existence for which I am eligible. I am yet, for example, to hear about an award for "the woman with the highest body mass index to make a first solo flight in 2008" or some such.

But I am keen on awards. They serve to not only honour the winner, but *encourager les autres*. One of the toughest awards to win is Journalist of the Year, because it is decided by a jury of journalists. This is why it was very pleasing that my colleague Gillian Tett was named "Journalist of the Year 2009" in March. The judges' citation declared that she had been "consistently in front of the curve as the world's economy went into meltdown".

It was a timely reminder to the outside world that the *Financial Times* is not staffed solely with white, male, Anglo-Saxon alumni of Balliol College, Oxford, but has some female talent as well. And it was encouraging for the *Financial Times* and the people who work there. Tett doesn't let the grass grow under her feet. A working mother, she has not only produced award-winning commentary on the crisis but has also written a book about the events that led to the world's credit markets seizing up. *Fool's Gold* is a worthy successor to her earlier book, *Saving the Sun*, and written in the style of one of my favourite books ever, Bryan Burrough's *Barbarians at the Gate*. By the time you get to the end of *Fool's Gold* you will think that you really know Blythe Masters (one of its protagonists).

Contrary to appearances, the *Financial Times* is full of over-achieving women. One, for example, is US managing editor, and another heads the *FT*'s commercial operations in Asia. And now, in conjunction with RBS Coutts, the *Financial Times* is establishing the Women in Asia Awards, to recognise the

106

contributions of women to business and society. The event
will be held in Hong Kong in October. I was in Asia to help
publicise these awards and while I sadly won't qualify, I want
to encourage any readers in the region to nominate entrants or
even apply themselves.

One of the reasons that career women should be honoured
is that they are often trying to manage a household and raise
a family at the same time. Tett said recently that her young
daughters had watched her book's progress with interest. The
older one had suggested that instead of writing about bankers,
her mother would do better to write about princesses, who were
much prettier.

I know some very attractive female bankers and am sure that
there are some very unattractive princesses around, although,
as I am not a big reader of *Hello!* magazine, I couldn't tell you
which. While I was in Hong Kong, I also did a book signing.
It does get a bit repetitive after a while and I barely looked up
as a succession of women thrust books under my nose and told
me their names. The 55th or so woman who appeared told me
her name was Autumn. Who names their child after a season,
for goodness sake? Scribbling away, I tried to be charming.
"What a lovely name," I said, not looking up. "It is the name
of the newest person to join our royal family. She's Canadian."
"I'm Canadian," the woman said, as I carried on writing.
"Gosh," I said, "it must be a more common name in Canada
than I realised." She then asked "Do you think I look like her?"
I turned and handed the book to a very pretty western girl who
barely looked old enough to be getting married. "No," I said.
"You are younger and prettier."
Needless to say, it was indeed her – Peter Phillips' wife. I blame
the *FT* – it is the only paper I read, and it rarely carries photos
of royalty. No royal-spotting awards for me, then.

## GIVE OVER, DARLING –
## 50% TAX WON'T DIG US OUT OF THIS HOLE
*May 15, 2009*
On April 22, the Chancellor of the Exchequer announced
The Budget. For those of you not living in the UK or who

prefer (wisely) not to know about these things, the role of the Budget is to provide an update on the state of the economy (in a word, dire) and the public finances (worse) and to present new forecasts for each, to set out the government's economic and fiscal objectives (as far as I can see, to stifle investment by small and medium-size companies), to report on the progress it has made toward achieving its objectives (like what?), and to explain the further steps it is taking to meet them (soak the rich). The record for the longest Budget speech is thought to be held by William Gladstone on April 18 1853, lasting four hours 45 minutes. Fortunately, this year's took slightly less long.

Much publicity has been given to the announcement in this year's Budget of an increase in higher rate tax on people who earn more than £150,000 a year in salary. This will rise from 40 per cent to 50 per cent next April and if you also take into account the removal of the tax-free allowance for higher earners and the increase in national insurance contributions, there are certain salary levels where people's marginal rate of tax will be in excess of 60 per cent. The government says, rightly, that these tax levels will affect a very small proportion of UK taxpayers. But it is almost certain that among them will be people who own businesses, and who we need to invest in these businesses.

I had a complete Budget meltdown last year about the move to a single rate of capital gains tax. Not because my rate, as an entrepreneur, had moved from 10 to 18 per cent, but because there was no longer any differential between someone sitting on their backside punting stocks on the internet and people like me who create jobs and invest in people. The argument went that the differential between the top rate of income tax (then 40 per cent) and the 10 per cent CGT rate was causing all sorts of people (mainly private equity) to dress up income as capital gains. Well, the differential then was 30 per cent. Now, it will be 32 per cent. How does that work?

But now we have a barefaced raid on our cash. It could not be clearer if the chancellor had dressed for his speech in camouflage with a safecracker in one hand and a bag marked "swag" in the other. From April 2010, dividends paid to people earning more than £150,000 will be taxed at 42.5 per cent. And also from that date, higher rate relief for pension contributions will be abolished. If I was a business owner who earned, or was likely to earn, £150,000 a year, what does that say to me? Remove money from your company now as dividends and pension contributions!

If entrepreneurs and business owners do remove money to reduce their likely tax bill, the money won't be in the companies and therefore available for investment. How does that help us out of this recession? And the worst is that I am not sure that any other government would do any better. The only people who are going to benefit from all this are tax planners. I suppose there is some justice in this, in that they are all bound to earn more than £150,000 a year and so will be paying for our schools and hospitals. All you single girls in the UK, go and find an accountant to marry, preferably one in tax (or recovery). The other people who might benefit, I suppose, are in the drinks industry, notwithstanding the extra few pence on a pint of beer in the Budget. The Chancellor of the Exchequer, by law, is allowed to drink alcohol to refresh himself during his speech. No other MP is allowed to bring alcohol into the chamber, at any time, not even if the speech does go for four hours and 45 minutes. I, however, will need a drink – or several – to recover from this Budget, and I suspect I may not be alone.

## LETS DO SOMETHING SPONTANEOUS! I'VE GOT A FREE AFTERNOON IN JULY
*May 23, 2009*

"I am amazed that you ever find the time for sex," Cost Centre #2 (age 14) said to me as we were out walking the dog.

This was a genuine observation on my hectic schedule rather than a bizarre attempt to broach a taboo subject. CC#2 had just declared that he never wanted to hear – and thought no child should ever have to hear – any reference whatsoever by his parents to the possibility that they were still sexually active. His comment on my schedule came at the end of this homily.

I couldn't really focus on responding (47 isn't that old/where do you think you came from?/most people's grandparents are still sexually active and so on) because I was caught up in wondering how we find time for anything.

Time is now the scarcest and most precious commodity I possess. You could argue that I have brought this situation upon myself by having three children, a career, two part-time jobs and various charitable interests. But I am not trying to work out why I am in this position. I am just reflecting that I now appear to have reached a stage where spontaneity is all but impossible, since so much of my life is planned well in advance.

And it's not just me. I called up my dentist on May 1 to book an appointment with the hygienist. I had planned to work from home on May 21 and thought half an hour with the hygienist – long overdue – would be a sensible use of my time. The next available appointment was in July. July! Is everyone in south Oxfordshire having their teeth scoured over the next few months? It must be the recession: no one is going on holiday this year; they're going to see the hygienist instead. Have they got nothing better to do? What about having more sex?

Then there is my latest lunch appointment. Towards the end of April, I was invited out to lunch by a business acquaintance. I don't like lunch because it takes up so much time in the middle of the day, but there's a recession on and therefore I can't use the time more wisely to go to the hygienist, so I agreed. Two days later, his secretary got in touch to offer me the choice of three dates. All of which were in July.

What is he doing every lunchtime from now until July? Going to the hygienist? This is someone who has worked for the same company for more than 25 years and so surely has got his life under control by now. (His previous job was selling advertising for Playboy in Paris. How much "selling" do you think that involved?) Granted, I did book tickets for the Test match against Australia last October, and I can recite all the key dates in the school calendar until December 2010, but I would hate to have mapped out so much of my life that the earliest I could meet up with someone was nearly two months hence. Moreover, July is a busy month, so finding time to go to the dental hygienist and have lunch with ex-employees of Playboy could prove tricky. There's Wimbledon, Henley, the Game Fair and the Cartier Polo to name but a few engagements that – recession or no recession – are in my diary for July.

Another event in July that I will definitely attend – albeit for the last time – is the 160th Royal Agricultural Show. When I was a student in the agriculture faculty at Newcastle University in the 1980s, this was the event that none of us would miss. Organised by the Royal Agricultural Society, it runs for four days, is attended by more than 100,000 visitors and is a logistical triumph as well as offering great shopping, the chance to catch up with friends in the members' bar, and an opportunity to see every agricultural innovation imaginable.

The show's trustees say that, in its current form, it is no longer economically viable. So, in July 2010 I will have some spare time. I shall schedule a visit to the dental hygienist – and, who knows, perhaps some sex.

## MY WORK COMES FIRST UNLESS IT'S MAKING THE BED
*May 30, 2009*

If you are a woman, do you know if you are adaptive? And no, I don't mean have you managed to adapt to your husband never putting the butter back in the fridge, like Michelle Obama, or never making the bed, like me.

Adaptive women, according to the London School of Economics sociologist Catherine Hakim, are women who want to combine work and family activities. And they gain qualifications with the intention of using them in their careers.

This does not strike me as a surprising theoretical discovery, and even without reading Hakim's work I would have guessed that most women fitted this description – indeed, she estimates that 60 per cent fall into the adaptive category. I, however, don't – I'm "work-centred". The main priority of this group (20 per cent of the total, according to Hakim) is employment or equivalent work in the public arena. Their qualifications are heavily focused on career advancement.

I am not a student of labour market economics and so had not come across Hakim until I shared a speaking engagement with her recently. I was interested in her attempts to classify women in developed economies (whom she recognises as being heterogeneous in their approach to work) in order to predict their response rate to labour market policies.

In particular, I liked her observation about the "home-centred" category, who account for the remaining 20 per cent of women, and their approach to qualifications. Home-centred women prefer not to work and gain qualifications, apparently, only for their "intellectual dowry". I can just see this. ("What would you prefer, darling? A Harvard MBA? Extensive postgraduate qualifications in microbiology? Shall I get myself called to the Bar?")

I wonder how Hakim would have categorised Gertrude Tennant. She died in 1918, at almost 100, just as the First World War was coming to an end. The daughter of a Royal Navy captain, Tennant had moved to France as a very young child and was educated there, famously falling in love with Flaubert before marrying a British MP 23 years her senior. Presumably she adapted, too, to his leaving the butter out of the fridge, or the 19th-century equivalent, because the marriage survived and she produced four children, but, as could have been expected, she was widowed in 1873.

Unlike Queen Victoria, who, when widowed, withdrew from public life, Tennant thrived on being unshackled from marriage. She established a salon at her house in London's Richmond Terrace. It was soon a meeting-place for such eminent Victorians as Gladstone, Ruskin, Tennyson, Browning and Wilde.

Personally, I would put the widowed Gertrude into the same Hakim category as myself. I can find no formal evidence of her gaining qualifications for any purpose, although she could apparently recite most of Shakespeare by heart. It's a bit late to ask her whether she learnt to do this to enhance her salons, or for an intellectual dowry. ("Darling, don't worry about your law degree, but if you could knock out a few sonnets that would be handy.") This weekend, Yale University Press is publishing a biography of Tennant written by David Waller, so I shall read it and see if I can view her through Hakim's eyes.

My approach to work is, I suspect, less heterogeneous than Hakim might think. Especially the work that married mothers of three do after they have finished paid work for the day. When you find yourself close to boiling point because you are putting the butter back in the fridge, or making the bed, while your husband is reviewing golf scores on the internet and your children are on the PlayStation, do you stop and ask yourself whether you are adaptive? Me neither. I'm just bloody furious.

## A PLAN TO ABOLISH SOCCER? I MUST BE DREAMING
*Jun 06, 2009*

I wake up to Radio 4 every morning. Sometimes I wonder if I am awake, or if I am just having a wonderful dream. Last month, I awoke to hear that the Conservative party had hinted that if it came to power in the next general election, it was likely to abolish soccer. Fantastic! I sat up in bed and prepared to break out the champagne, no matter the time of day. My vote was theirs.

I have never been a fan of soccer, or, to give it its proper name, association football. I have never seen the appeal of a sport where so few goals are scored. As I understand it, it is possible to watch an entire 90-minute game with no score. Then they might have another 30 minutes for extra time – which can also end with no score. And after that, if they need a result to decide a knock-out competition, they have a penalty shoot-out, which takes just a few minutes. Why not cut to the chase and do that at the beginning? It would save us all a lot of time.

As I write this, thousands of people have returned from Rome after watching the most famous football team in the world take on the Spanish (or more precisely, the Catalans, who hate to be lumped in with the rest of Spain). Historically, we have usually confronted Spain at sea; Elizabeth I created an entire navy for the purpose. Why it was necessary to travel to Rome, I have no idea. And even for those who made the journey, the Armada would have been more exciting – there were only two goals in an hour and a half of football – one in the 10th minute and the other 20 minutes before the end.

Sadly, neither was scored by Manchester United. They conceded goals to the unlikely sounding duo Eto'o and Messi, and so fared rather worse than Sir Francis Drake in 1588. Even more sadly, as I sat in bed preparing to celebrate the demise of this irksome sport, I realised I had misunderstood the radio report. The Conservatives, it seems, might in fact be intending to abolish Soca, the Serious Organised Crime Agency. I don't know why – maybe we don't have any serious organised crime any more?

It's an education, Radio 4. This morning, I woke up to discover that a study of 1,000 expectant mothers has shown that relaxation and breathing techniques do not reduce the need for pain relief during labour. The women involved had attended one of two classes: the first taught natural coping methods, the other emphasised pain relief. But the study found no difference in the use of epidurals between the women when they went into labour.

I thought I was dreaming again. How was this news? Why did 500 Swedish women waste their time learning how to relax and breathe? Any fool could have predicted that, when the time came to deliver a baby, they would all be yelling for drugs. Childbirth hurts. I know: I have had three children. And even before I had the first, I didn't faff around learning how to relax and breathe. I was working far too hard to relax, and I breathe anyway – that's how I stay alive.

I did briefly attend antenatal classes in 1989. I didn't learn much, but gained a lifelong friend. We both departed the classes prematurely; I was expelled and she had her child so prematurely that the classes had not finished. I suspect we both had better things to do than learn how to breathe through labour, and we probably still do. In her case, she has just written a best-selling book on must-see museums in China.

My advice on how to deal with pain in childbirth is quite simple – have an epidural line put in at eight months and walk around with it. There is no, I repeat, no point in enduring pain of any kind. Just as there is no point in watching 90 minutes of association football, in Rome or anywhere else. Do you want my vote, David Cameron? Then never mind about Soca, abolish soccer.

## DON'T LET SOBER COMPANY RESULTS DAMPEN A BOOZY MEETING
*Jun 27, 2009*

I don't employ many men. Two, to be precise. I should probably employ more because they are extremely handy, especially when it comes to changing light bulbs or carrying large containers of water upstairs.

These days our main business employs 16 people and so the two males have 14 female colleagues. It takes a brave man to come to work with all these women each day, and an even braver one to go away with them for a night or two. We usually organise an off-site meeting for the senior team once a year to discuss company strategy. Afterwards, the rest of our colleagues join us for dinner and some socialising, which gives everyone a chance to escape the office and spend some time with colleagues when there's no work to be done.

Last year, after the best 12 months the business has had, we decamped to the Four Seasons in Hampshire – the lap of luxury, with Frette sheets and in-room satellite TV. This year, we were looking for an option that was cheaper but still a treat: not easy. Fortunately my Ducal Girlfriend has just fitted out one of the rooms in her house with audio-visual kit for exactly our kind of event, so off we went.

It is a good thing for all businesses to stop once a year, reflect on the past 12 months and look ahead to the next 12 and more. Usually, I present the year's financial results at the start, and I did so again this time. We haven't had our most stellar year and although we remain cash-positive and profitable the figures didn't make for very happy reading, especially when set against the previous year.

So I delivered two other presentations alongside the numbers.

The first was a long series of photographs of all the people our business had worked with over the past year. Businesses are about making money but all their transactions involve people; the human story is a powerful complement to the financial story. Second, I dug out pictures of ourselves from the past 12 months – from our non-winning netball team to our Christmas party – and had the sequence set to music. People, not just profits.

DG may be a friend, but this was a commercial transaction. Belvoir Castle doesn't have Frette sheets or in-room satellite TV, but then it doesn't cost as much as the Four Seasons. It does, however, have four-poster beds and art worth several millions of pounds on the walls, and it is so large that during the day, when there were schools visiting and other things going on, it still felt as if we had the place to ourselves. In the evenings, we really did. And, best of all, it has a karaoke machine, which we put to good use in the library after dinner in the State Dining Room.

DG gave rousing on-message speech to the troops, which was so impressive that I suggested she join the motivational speaking circuit. She (a former Guildhall School of Music and Drama student) then kicked off the karaoke for us with "Daydream Believer" by the Monkees. They don't include a singing duchess in the price at the Four Seasons.

But she had long departed for bed when we hit the 1am crisis: we ran out of drink. This can be very demotivating for a team in full karaoke mode and so I volunteered to find fresh supplies.

It was at this point that I remembered why we employ men. They are very useful for accompanying you through dark, echoing castle hallways with suits of armour lining the walls as you search for (a) light switches and (b) chilled white wine. We eventually found our way through a kitchen into the restaurant that is used by the public. The fridge contained six bottles of wine that were all partially open, presumably to be sold by the glass. We carried them back to the library to be greeted with a heroes' welcome. Shared memories and men. Both very useful for any business.

## THE CHANGE THAT NO PARENT WANTS TO MAKE
*Jul 04, 2009*

*"Vale, heroum filii."* I hate saying goodbye, even in Latin. It is hard wrenching yourself away from a place where you feel at home, where the buildings are familiar, the teachers are supportive, you have lots of friends and where you believe you have been part of a pre-eminent educational establishment. And that's just how you feel as a parent. Imagine how your child must feel.

Because Moneypenny plc has not been immune to the recession, the Cost Centres are about to become the Reduced Cost Centres. Managing a business is one long risk-assessment exercise, and the question CEOs have been asking themselves in this recession is: what are the risks of continuing to spend at current levels while revenue plummets? Finance departments have been modelling and remodelling to show what would happen if sales fell to 2006 levels, or worse. Running a family is just the same – what are the risks if bonuses and dividends are not forthcoming for the next few years? In our case it would have meant that CC#2 might well have had to come out of school halfway through his GCSE syllabus, and changing school at that point is very tough. So we decided to eliminate that risk by removing him from his senior boarding school after only a year and sending him to the local selective day school. And his younger brother is coming out of his heinously expensive prep school and being sent back to the local village school where he started his education.

CC#1 is not immune from all this; he is off to university this autumn and we have combined cost management with a revised incentive scheme. We will not pay his fees, so he will have to take out a loan. But if he returns after three years with the same class of degree as me, or better, we will write him a cheque to cover the fees.

These are all significant changes, and, like the ones I oversaw at the office earlier this year, they were undertaken with a heavy heart and, I admit, more than a few tears. At the board meeting to discuss the restructuring (at our dinner table) Mr M advanced argument after argument for continuing to outsource the CCs to boarding school (what we have done for one we ought to do for the others etc etc). But in this economic environment, there are no sacred cows, and while I agree that CC#2 was getting what is probably the best education money can buy, was it really going to deliver him a three times better result in life than the next best alternative? Because, make no mistake, it costs three times as much. I also realised that most of the reasons that Mr M and I felt so sad about CC#2 in particular were on our own account, not his. We have felt privileged to co-parent and educate our children in a historic school with fantastic teaching staff. It is very sad to have to say goodbye.

But CC#2 is a diligent and ambitious student, who will succeed wherever he studies. And we are not the only people to review our personal expenditure. At every level, the people I know are cutting back, although all things are relative. Mr M and I dined recently at the home of a man who has more people on his personal payroll (crew for the yacht, gardeners for the house in France and so on) than I do in my business. But the cook has gone, and our host barbecued for us, and sent his wife out to buy the cheese. (And still found time to show off the lighting system in his basement loo – what is it about boys and toys?)

The rich and/or famous are not immune. Our friends the Famous Couple celebrated their 10th wedding anniversary the other day. They told guests to bring their own tables, chairs and cutlery for a picnic dinner and found the ultimate boy with a toy – a hedge fund manager with a disco kit – to provide the 1980s music. Lots of parents will have to make tough choices in this recession, and I hope boys, not just ours, will look back and realise that, wherever they went to school, they are still *heroum filii*.

## 12,000 MILES IN A WEEKEND?
### THERE'S NETWORKING TO BE DONE
*Jul 11, 2009*

Four days before the British & Irish Lions were due to play the Springboks in the second Test in Pretoria, I received an invitation to attend. The only girl in a party of six. Three days in South Africa, over a weekend, would require extensive diary rearrangements and (as we were expecting guests) Mr M to locate the linen cupboard.

I couldn't possibly accept. Who would change the sheets, do the laundry, the shopping and the cooking at the weekend if I pushed off to a rugby match 6,000 miles away? On the other hand, who would do all that if I didn't go to the game? Yes, me. I rang back and accepted immediately.

Mr M evinced total disbelief. Why would five men want to go to a rugby match with me? Why not? I had a very good time, as it happens. Not only was the rugby very exciting but it was a very social event. I was only immobilised for an hour and a half in the Loftus stadium; the rest of the time I was networking furiously. From newspaper editors to finance directors, they were all there. The question is not why did I go; it's why had I never been before.

I did struggle a bit with the rules of rugby union. While the atmosphere at a live sporting fixture is impossible to recreate in your living room, at least there you see the action up close, plus you usually have someone on hand to explain what's going on. The Lions led at the end of the first half, and right at the end of the second it looked as if the match was going to be a draw, which would have set the series up nicely for the third and final encounter. But no. For some reason South Africa were awarded a penalty – and they kicked it straight between the posts.

The striking thing about the Springboks was how few black players they have. More than 20 years after Nelson Mandela walked free from prison, the national rugby team still consists mainly of white players. On the other hand, the national South African football team, Bafana Bafana, is almost entirely black – an exception being a chap called Matthew Booth.

I guess that while rugby remains a game played by privileged children you can't expect much change. Which is why I was pleased to read in the match programme that the Lions' principal sponsor, HSBC, has been supporting a scheme to introduce rugby to children in South Africa's townships. Some 80 per cent of the children who have participated in the

programme have never played rugby before. Maybe by the
time the Lions return to South Africa, in a few years, it will
have helped to ensure the team reflects the racial balance of the
country a little better.

Of course, the real reason HSBC was in the news that weekend
was not its rugby sponsorship, but because its chairman,
Stephen Green, had just published a book. *Good Value* (let's
put a disclaimer out right now: this is published by Penguin, a
Pearson company) doesn't mention rugby. But given the state
of the world economy, any book subtitled *Reflections on Money,
Morality and an Uncertain World* and which is only 250 pages
long should, in my opinion, expect a strong following. Not
many of my travelling companions had read it, but they all read
the reviews on the plane back, lounging around on the overnight
flight in their pyjamas. (Want to see what other people's
husbands wear in bed? Go on an overnight flight with them.)
These reviews were far more uplifting than the reports of the
game. I didn't even read those, which is why it took me another
week to discover why that penalty had been awarded. (Why
can't you tackle someone when he is up in the air?) Instead, I
went to South Africa and back with my nose in Jeremy Pratt's
gripping 400-page tome *The Private Pilot's Licence Course:
Navigation & Meteorology*, now in its third edition, fourth
reprint. Now that was really good value.

FROM BLACKBERRYS TO BAKING –
SHORTCUTS FOR THE TIME POOR
*Jul 18, 2009*
Tips and tricks. I am always keen to learn about things that
might save me time. People often ask me how I manage
everything – the business, the writing, the teaching, the charity
work, the three Cost Centres. Oh, and a husband who really
cannot understand why people need to wear top hats to go to
Royal Ascot. ("I look like an undertaker/what do the British
think they are playing at/I could have bought a new driver for
the price of this hat", etc.)

My top tip for busy working women is to learn from other

people about how to save time. I will forever be grateful to the person (herself a working mother) who taught me that by pressing the letter "t" at any time on your BlackBerry you go straight to the top of the e-mail pile, or, if you are in an e-mail, straight to the top of the e-mail itself. So, here are two of my own top tips for time-saving if, like me, you are trying to multitask faster than a Cray computer. I have also added my personal favourite websites from the Mrs M black book.

First, take a laptop to the hairdresser, especially when you are having your colour done. The wonderful thing about hairdressers is that there are power points at every seat. I recognise that this only applies to women, and it is also a credit crunch tip – when we start to leave the recession I will return to the ultimate time-saving measure with hair, which is to have someone come to the office. In London, this also works with manicures and other beauty treatments. Try www.perfectlyathome.com.

Second, take taxis from time to time instead of (a) the tube or (b) driving yourself. This allows you to make those three extra telephone calls that you wouldn't otherwise have time for. My children, my parents, the business call that is not time-sensitive but probably reputation-building – these are all beneficiaries from being above ground and not driving myself. It might cost money but the gain will be disproportionate. As the recession ends, have yourself driven regularly – not many businesses can justify a full-time driver but chauffeurs cost less than you think. Any evening with more than two must-be-seen-at drinks parties justifies the expense: no need to check your coat, you can leave your bag in the car, as well as reserve supplies of business cards and spare pairs of tights, and you can look generous by offering to drive people home in something better than a mini-cab. Try www.meridianchauffeurs.com. (And, if you run out of spare pairs of tights, have them sent to the office with www.mytights.com.)

I think you get the picture. Please do send me your own time-saving measures – as I said, I love to learn! One of my colleagues, another busy working mother, sent us all an e-mail today that showed not only a worrying preoccupation with baking but, more generously, how much we all think of trying to save each other time. "I made these last night between putting my Cost Centre to bed, cooking for my in-laws, packing for our holiday and doing some work!" She was referring to some brownies.

Now, I am not a brownie-baking sort of mother – what is Marks and Spencer for? – but here is my, or rather her, final time-saving tip.

Oven at 180°C; 8in cake tin, buttered and lined.

Slowly melt together 185g dark chocolate and 185g butter.

Mix in 200g sugar (I use 100g brown and 100g caster), plus 1 tsp vanilla essence.

Beat in 3 large eggs.

Mix in 125g of plain flour.

Mix in one small bag of pecans, lightly crushed by hand as you drop them in.

Pour into tin and bake for 20-25 minutes.

You can double the recipe and bake in a shallow roasting tin. Delicious!

## GLYNDEBOURNE HAS MANY CHARMS – AND THE OPERA'S GOOD TOO
*Jul 25, 2009*

Rampant rabbits take over Sussex beauty spot. No, this is not an extra chapter in *Watership Down*, but my interpretation of Glyndebourne's staging of Purcell's *The Fairy Queen*. Just before the production pauses for the long interval (an hour and 20 minutes, during which the opera-goers have dinner) the stage is filled with cartoon-like bunnies simulating copulation, all perfectly choreographed and looking like they had sprung straight from Nickelodeon.

I never fail to be surprised by opera. I am not an opera buff and need good reasons to attend. In this instance, it was an invitation from a couple I enjoy seeing, to a location that is very beautiful, in the company of others whom I knew I would find stimulating. The music was a bonus.

This could be the story of the English summer. Someone observed to me recently that this season of the year is about walls, doors and food. Take a wall, any wall, put a door in it, make it difficult to get a ticket to go through the door, and put smart food and drink on the other side. People will pay a fortune to get through that door, irrespective of what is happening – sport, opera, even a flower show. And they will pay up more than once a season!

This can lead to very tricky situations. My friend with a VCH (Very Clever Husband) was invited with him to Glyndebourne recently to see *Falstaff*. It's a great production, and they were the guests of lovely people, so they accepted – despite having already seen the production earlier in the season. During dinner, VCH was asked by his hosts if he had been to Glyndebourne already that season. "Yes," he truthfully replied. "And what did you see?" he was asked.

At this point VCH's brain, which fortunately operates at very high speed, had to perform a large number of simultaneous calculations even more rapidly than usual. What should he say? Should he admit to having already seen *Falstaff*? Would that be offensive? If not *Falstaff*, what else should he say that he had seen? What else had been on? Was there time to reach for the programme and check?

He intimated that they had seen something else. It turned out that his hosts had also been to Glyndebourne earlier in the season and had seen the other production. Had he enjoyed it? At this point even VCH realised that he needed his Very Supportive Wife to bail him out and turn the conversation away from what happened in the second act of an opera he had not seen.

The surprising thing about Glyndebourne is not how many people go to the same production more than once a season, but how the company puts on such spectacular productions without government subsidy. Even if you are not an opera fan, go and wonder at this – in an age when taxpayers' money goes on more and more bizarre things, it is worthy of note.

However, I struggled to get into *The Fairy Queen* – even with the rampant rabbits. It got easier after the interval, during which

I was briefed by one of my fellow guests on what *Restoration* audiences would have expected and enjoyed. By the second act I was imagining myself back in the latter half of the 17th century and enjoyed it a lot more, especially the mournful lament of a widow for her husband. (Personally, I am not sure I would have wept for so long. At least she would no longer have to pick up his laundry from the bedroom floor.)

As the novelist Jeanette Winterson says: "Glyndebourne is more than a night at the opera; it is music for the rest of your life." She has recently edited *Midsummer Nights*, a book of short stories by a range of authors to celebrate the festival's 75th birthday, which I am about to start reading. The blurb on it says that "the results range from comic delights to moving dissections of relationships". Yes, but will it have rampant rabbits?

## MY READERS OFFER SUPPORT - AND LATIN LESSONS - IN TOUGH TIMES
*Aug 01, 2009*

Reader feedback: always welcome, never dull. Columnists may moan occasionally about the size of their postbag, but the truth is we like it really. It reminds us that someone out there is reading our views on life, however trivial they are, and bothering to respond. A reader recently told me that "I may not always agree with your columns", but went on to praise our decision to remove our two younger children, Cost Centres #2 and #3 (or rather, Reduced Cost Centres), from their heinously expensive private schools and send them to local ones. This reader, who sends her own CC to a large, local state primary school, said: "We have never regretted her going there for one moment. She has a lot of fun and, in terms of academic achievement, she and her schoolmates are more than holding their own against their more expensively educated out-of-school friends. They also have the advantage of a full social life on their doorstep!"

Such encouragement was typical of almost every e-mail I received. Sure, I had a couple of more cynical correspondents, and even one from a regular reader of *Significance*, a quarterly journal published under the supervision of the Royal Statistical Society. The aim of *Significance*, apparently, is "to communicate and demonstrate in an entertaining and thought-provoking way the practical use of statistics". Golly.

In the June 2009 issue, there was a paper entitled "What have private schools done for (some of) us?", written by Professor Francis Green and three other worthy individuals. In this, they estimate that, for a data set of 10,000 people, if all other factors are equal (such as family background), students who attend private school will earn more than 20 per cent more over their lifetime than their state-educated peers. So, I could be about to reduce the Cost Centres' ability to become Profit Centres!

Apart from those e-mails, and another correcting my Latin (always good to know that Latin scholars are reading *FT Weekend*), the remainder have been very encouraging. "Welcome to the real world" has been the theme. "The three CCs will survive and prosper – children are so resilient," one reader said. Another particularly cheering e-mail came from a reader in his early twenties who had been through a very similar experience, from the child's perspective. He said it had been a difficult adjustment at first, but it had worked out well in the end and he had been fine.

I had expected a big postbag from our school decision. What I had not expected was the tsunami of correspondence over my comments about South African rugby and the apparent lack of black representation in the national team. "Surely that is a matter for the coaches, rugby players and the selection committee of South Africa to decide, and to respond to the question [of] whether it is more important to have a politically correct approach to selection based on ethnic quotas, or a team selected from the best available players, one that can train together, work together, and function and operate to win in future international contests." This represented the considered and thoughtful end of the spectrum. The other end can be summed up by the reader who didn't even write in the body of the e-mail, but said in the subject line: "Get over it and quit your ridiculous liberal ideology."

Fortunately, a few of you also wrote in to explain the rules
of rugby, including a German reader who said the sport had
been explained to him by some Australian friends. But the
greatest number of e-mails came from people who realised that
I had not checked one important fact. I hereby apologise, and
acknowledge that the 20th anniversary of Nelson Mandela's
release from prison is not until February. Thank you, readers,
for that feedback. It is always welcome.

AT LAST, SOMETHING TO SMILE ABOUT AT THE DENTIST
*Aug 08, 2009*
Teeth can be a pain. And how. In adult life, I have been
meticulous about going to the dentist for check-ups and have
never been in dire physical pain on account of a tooth, although
I had a few fillings when I was a teenager. I am English,
of course, and grew up at a time when parents did not send
their offspring routinely to the orthodontist. (My children, by
contrast, have been or will go – Cost Centre #1 has a dazzling
smile that cost £2,500.) So, while I am a bit self-conscious
about my smile on aesthetic grounds, I have not been worried
about its health.

Then this year I cracked a very old filling, quite badly, and I
thought I was going to need to have the tooth crowned. Groan.
I am not good at spending time out of the office and I could
see that this was going to need two visits. On the first, I knew I
would have an injection of anaesthetic, the dodgy filling would
be removed and the cavity cleaned, an impression taken, and
a temporary restoration put on. A dental technician in a lab
somewhere would make the crown, and I would return about
two weeks later to have another injection, so that the temporary
fix could be prised off (if it hadn't fallen out already) and the
permanent one fitted.

This is especially bad when you consider that I have a phobia
of needles. Years ago, when having an amniocentesis for CC#2
in Hong Kong, the doctor produced the biggest needle I had
ever seen. I was off the consulting bed and down the hall before

he could say "lie still please". After the nurse and Mr M had
persuaded me to return, the doctor looked at my robust frame
and said: "You had better get used to needles – or lose weight.
You are almost certainly going to end up diabetic." What a
delightful man.

So, the prospects of two visits and two injections did not fill
me with enthusiasm. But as it turned out I needn't have worried
– the dentist told me that it would only require one visit, one
injection and no technicians. I was talking to the dentist of
the future. He told me he was going to remove the cracked
filling and clean the cavity out but then, instead of putting in a
temporary fix, he was going to photograph the cavity using a
3D camera, play around with the image on a screen to refine the
shape using something that looked like CAD software, and then
mill the required filling immediately – in the next room, using
an industrial-diamond-tipped, computer-driven tool. While this
was going on, for just 15 minutes or so, I would put my feet up
and read *Hello!*

It turns out that this process was invented nearly 30 years ago
by some enterprising folk at the University of Zurich, and the
technology is called CEREC. This is an acronym for Chairside
Economical Restoration of Esthetic Ceramics. (No wonder they
don't use its full name. And is "esthetic" a real word?)
Siemens acquired the licence to develop and manufacture the
equipment in 1986, and then in 1997 its dental division was sold
to a private equity-backed buyout and renamed Sirona. After
a reverse takeover in 2006 of a US "intra-oral radiographic
imaging specialist" (who dreams up these descriptions?), Sirona
acquired a listing on Nasdaq. The company even has a female
finance director, Simone Blank, who is smiling on the website,
her gleaming white teeth on display. And she is not American
– she is German!

I have been registered with my dentist since 1998, when he
was young and single and keen to push the frontiers of dentistry.
He is now married with children, but still keen on those
frontiers, and he is one of the few dentists in the UK to have
had a CEREC machine (and several versions thereof) almost

from the beginning. From a lab bench in Zurich to a market town in South Oxfordshire – and now the world. Innovation is wonderful, isn't it?

## EVEN HIGH-FLYERS WANT TO COME DOWN TO EARTH
*Aug 15, 2009*

Lost in Oxfordshire. It was a rainy Saturday, and I was fed up and frustrated because I could not find my way to where I was going. I was on my own, and my mobile hadn't got a signal. I had a map, but no GPS. Finally, I decided to give up and go home – except that even with the map I couldn't work out where home was. This was because I was at 2,000ft in a little single-engine aeroplane, surrounded by clouds that showed no sign of disappearing.

I had been "lost" before but, on that occasion, it was deliberate. I had had an instructor on board who had (a) sneakily put a handheld radio next to the compass to make sure I went in a totally different direction to my planned route, and (b) had a GPS in his flight bag in case he got lost too. Then I had to go through my carefully rehearsed "lost" drills, which included everything from looking at the map to calling up the emergency frequency and asking for a radar fix. But this time I really was lost.

Fortunately, the weather was much better when I flew myself to the CLA Game Fair last month, and I managed not to get lost. A cracking tailwind meant that Oxford to Leicestershire took a brisk 29 minutes, there were no clouds, East Midlands air traffic control looked after me splendidly, and the £5 landing fee at Langar seemed more than reasonable. My Ducal Girlfriend was hosting the 2009 fair and she was my hostess too, for I holed up in her house for the duration of the event, an annual affair that rotates between various stately homes, and showcases the best of British hunting, shooting and fishing.

As I was well down the pecking order of important guests in DG's castle, I was billeted in a turret up a flight of stairs designed to give me so much exercise that I was in danger of becoming as slender as DG herself. My room had twin beds so I immediately called up my Most Glamorous Girlfriend, who was working at the fair for a leading land agent, and upgraded her from the Premier Inn. High in our turret, we had the privilege of sharing a bathroom with the guests in the adjacent room; on the first night this was a very attractive male Tory MP, who had clearly been sent to the turret to deflect any accusations of lavish hospitality. He cautioned us at dinner that he liked his bathrooms neat and tidy – "not the way girls usually leave them". Hmm.

Mr M did not accompany me, but he too was sharing bathrooms with MPs. He had been drafted in to play with the Parliamentary Golfing Society – far more appealing than looking at shotguns, watching working dogs and hanging out at MGG's stand.

With MGG busy, and DG zooming around in an official golf cart presenting prizes and visiting stands, I was left to myself and fulfilled a long-held ambition – I learnt to fly-fish. The Game Angling Instructors Association offers free tuition every year at the fair and, after 45 minutes of single-handed casting, I rushed off to buy my very own (credit crunch price) rod and reel. Tying your own flies strikes me as up there with baking your own bread or making your own pasta, so I took myself off to the Salmon and Trout Association stand and bought some ready-made ones. Don't they have great names? I rather fancied a set of Montana Nymphs (I am sure every girl has an inner Montana Nymph dying to get out), but was told they were inappropriate for river fishing. Shame.

It rained on and off at the fair and I did get very tired, but I didn't get lost – I just had to look up to see where the castle was. That doesn't work when you are lost and surrounded by clouds at 2,000ft. Then you have to call up Oxford ATC and ask them what heading to set to get home. In future, if the weather looks dodgy, I shall go fly-fishing instead.

## A HEALTHY DOSE OF SCEPTICISM – FAR MORE USE THAN ANTIVIRALS
*Aug 22, 2009*

Have you had swine flu? If you read the newspapers and watch TV, especially in the UK, you would think that all 60 million of us were either infected or about to be. To the best of my knowledge I have not had swine flu (although I did have a nasty cough for a couple of weeks not long ago). Neither have the Cost Centres. Or have they? I suspect we may never know. Although there have been some deaths among those who have caught H1N1, as it is more properly known, in the UK they have mostly been people who had other things wrong with them already. Most of those who catch it seem to be (a) young and (b) suffer very few symptoms and get better very quickly. Should we really all be so very worried? And should we all be swallowing Tamiflu?

I suspect not. This is because, while antivirals have been shown to shorten the duration of the illness, to benefit from them you have to be taking the medication within 48 hours of getting sick. By the time most parents have worked out that their children might have swine flu and got them to a doctor, let alone sent a throat swab off to the lab and had the results, the crucial period has passed.

So the government has bought up the nation's entire stock of the antiviral Tamiflu and made it available via the internet and a telephone hotline. As a result, legions of people are taking Tamiflu in the UK. Can this be a good thing? Not only are we developing a resistance to the drug just before winter arrives and with it a probably much greater outbreak, it also makes a lot of people who take it feel wretched. As the manufacturers say on the product website: "The most common side effects of Tamiflu are mild to moderate nausea and vomiting."

My Medical Girlfriend has a private general practice in Oxford, a city with lots of young people, and so she has been super-busy of late. She has had to make lots of house calls as people are naturally wary of venturing forth with children whom they suspect should be in isolation. I have pointed out to her that she should be jolly grateful to whoever brought H1N1 to the UK – it has meant that she has been out to visit far more people than she would normally get to, and every household she visits is another potential advocate for her service. Having spent many years in Australia and London before that, she has had to start her business from scratch. What better than a swine flu pandemic to persuade consumers to sample her services?

Of course, until the government hotline/website opened, MG was rather handicapped by the NHS monopoly on supplies of Tamiflu. Even when she thought that the patients would benefit, she could not prescribe it. As a private GP, if she diagnosed a case of H1N1 after NHS surgery hours, she had to call out the (overworked) out-of-hours NHS service if the patient needed Tamiflu. I can understand the government wanting to make it available to all, and to prevent a black market in the drug, but surely it should be possible to license some private GPs?

MG is a very longstanding friend who assisted at the birth of CC#2. (CCs 1 & 2, born as they were of a mother obsessed with the capital markets and a father obsessed with cricket, were appropriately brought into the world by the late Peter Saunders, obstetrician, wicketkeeper and brother of the only person I have ever heard of who recovered from Alzheimer's.) The only thing she has ever prescribed for me is a new bread knife, about 10 years ago. It is true that I am not good at selecting kitchen implements and had never given my bread knife a thought until MG outlined to me in some detail why a good one is essential. Precautionary doses of Tamiflu or a decent bread knife? I know which one I reckon brings the greater benefit. Thank you, doctor.

## ASK ME MY AGE ON LIVE RADIO – HOW DARE THEY?
*Aug 29, 2009*

I am not ageist. I have friends and colleagues older and younger than me, and their age has no effect on my hiring decisions, firing decisions, or on how much I seek or enjoy their company. It is true that as the years go by I prefer the company of ever-older men, and these days anyone asking me out for lunch or dinner has to be pretty well starting their seventh decade before they are likely to be interesting enough for me to want to spend a whole evening with them. (There are honourable exceptions, including the 45-year-old hedge fund manager who recently squired me to Harry's Bar. Even if I did feel like his granny.)

I am energist, though. I find life such an exciting journey and crammed with so many things worth doing and seeing, that people who sit around doing nothing much, especially those who have no excuse, irritate me greatly. Cost Centre #1, who is busy writing his first book and determined to find a publisher before the end of his first year at university, tells me that in it he has included a discussion about his theory that apathy is the curse of the middle class. I have not seen the manuscript (there's a surprise) but apparently his argument is that he and his generation have suffered from being enclosed in a "gilded cage" of overprovision by their parents that has left them unused to having to achieve for themselves.

Personally, I know plenty of young people with lots of get up and go – and plenty of older people, too. My solution to needing energy is to exercise as regularly as I can, which makes me feel better and allows me to sleep fewer – and better quality – hours. As regular readers know, I work out at a boxing gym, and when it was announced recently that the International Olympic Committee was going to grant Olympic sport status to women's boxing, I was asked to give my views on a live radio show on BBC Radio Oxford.

I had 30 minutes' notice of this and took the call in the ticket office of Paddington Station, so I didn't have time to Google my interviewer, Bill Heine. After asking me my views on the IOC decision he then asked how old I was! I was taken slightly aback – is that a suitable question to ask a lady live on air? I admitted to being 47 and then pointed out that whatever sex you are, boxing is something you can do at 17 or 57. I certainly won't be aiming for an Olympic place, I never box competitively, and I can't see why my age should have a bearing on my views on the suitability of women boxing at the Olympics. How dare he? As it was radio, I probably should have just lied and said I was 35. I could also have said I was thin – who would know? You can live out (almost) all your fantasies on radio.

How old is Mr Heine, anyway? I called up the BBC and asked them, as it does not appear anywhere on the internet, not even on his Wikipedia entry. Bill Heine is something of an Oxford legend, a US citizen who came to the UK to study as a postgraduate student in the decade that I was born, and has never left. He is probably most famous for living in a house in Headington with a 25ft fibreglass shark embedded in its roof.

The answer, by the way, is that he is 64. Why does the BBC not make more of this? If I were them, I would have plastered it all over the internet, a strong counter-argument to those who called them ageist for retiring Arlene Phillips from Strictly Come Dancing. And Mr Heine comes from a country where people run the Federal Reserve Bank until three weeks short of their 80th birthday, so I assume he plans to go on working for a while.

While I have never met him, he doesn't seem to be short of energy. And he is in his seventh decade! Sounds like a suitable dinner companion to me.

## How to keep young guns happy in the holidays
*Sep 05, 2009*

I didn't expect to hit anything. Apart from one charity day I have not used my shotguns all year; the first six months were spent working round the clock in response to the recession. And since the business climate has improved (we noticed a watershed in June, although it's early days yet) no opportunity has presented itself. But I have discovered that my village, to which we moved last September, has a clay shooting club that operates for two hours a week. It leases its field from the council and is entirely member-run.

The club is right next to a private air strip. How many villages in England sport a clay shooting club next to a private air strip? And there is a boxing gym in the next village, only a mile away. I cannot imagine why I ever wanted to live anywhere else. The air strip also has hangar space for rent (it is always good to have aspirations).

The partridge season opened this week, so I needed some practice. Cost Centre #2 is currently a better shot than me. He and his best friend, a lovely German boy we have known for years, recently spent a week on an estate in Lincolnshire helping to prepare it for the game season.

Had you ever wondered what to do with bored 14- and 15-year-olds in the middle of the summer, here's your answer. Send them off to help take delivery of pheasants (which arrive in boxes of 30), prepare their pens (mending fences, clearing foliage, sorting out water and grain) and then spend their evenings outdoors with torches and .22 rifles getting rid of any vermin that look likely to dine out on the new arrivals. Add in some pigeon and rabbit shooting, then some lessons in how to pluck/skin and cook, and you will get the picture. No wonder they called after a few days to ask if they could extend their stay.

CC#2's absence relieved me of having to answer his continual questions. And he is not the only one; CC#3 is starting to develop a keen line of questioning. The most recent was to ask me how his oldest brother would ever pay back the student loan he is about to take out. Answer: the government will reclaim it from him once he earns more than £15,000 pa, but goodness knows when that will be, not least because he currently plans to earn a living writing screenplays! But at least I could answer that question; CC#2, as usual, asks much more difficult ones. This weekend he wanted to know, during a two-hour hike we took together, why cows had such complicated digestive systems. Answer – I definitely don't know, I don't even have Biology O-level, why don't you save that question for God when you get there, and in the meantime consult the internet?

He did consult the internet the previous week, when, home alone, he decided to cook macaroni cheese. Shelves of cookery books were left to collect dust while he Googled a recipe. I was impressed with this initiative, but have been told that he is not pleased about accepting my praise – apparently cooking is something that 14-year-olds don't do if they are cool. What do they do? Lines of coke? Cooking seems to me to be a very useful occupation for someone that age.

There were no 14-year-olds in evidence at my local clay shooting club, where I was the youngest person present by quite some years. At the end of the 90 minutes or so shooting time, everyone set to and packed up the equipment, while I and a few others were put to good use scouring the field to retrieve any clays that had fallen without breaking, so that they could be reused. I like that approach to recycling and happily brought back the piles and piles that I had missed. Because, as I had predicted, I didn't hit much.

### THE STRANGE CASE OF THE SUSPICIOUS UNDERPANTS
*Sep 12, 2009*

Cream and white. A lot of cream and white. That is how my Single Girlfriend described the house that we had been invited to. I do not usually require details of soft furnishings before I accept an invitation, but her intelligence (she has visited herself) was in response to an earlier invite to Cost Centre #3. CC#3 is a 10-year-old boy. Nothing like one's children (unescorted) to make or break your reputation when they are in close proximity to cream-and-white soft furnishings.

But then we were invited – sans children – to the same house. Mr M declined to go (key golf match). More fool him. Our host had generously provided all the hallmarks of an anti-credit crunch St Tropez weekend – private jet from London City and then a couple of EC-130s to pick us up from Toulon and put us down in the back garden. I was still at my desk at noon; by 5pm UK time I had unpacked, had a glass of champagne and was in the pool. But as I got out of the pool and covered myself in a cotton wrap (my legs do not bear inspection), disaster struck.

I sat down to chat to some fellow guests and sip another glass of champagne. Half an hour later, getting up to go and dress for dinner, I realised that I had sat in a non-colourfast wrap on a chair covered in cream cushions – leaving behind a prominent pink mark. Forget CC#3 – his mother had wrecked the soft furnishings within an hour of arrival. I spirited the cushion away to the kitchen where the staff took over and it was back on the chair the next day, our host seemingly unknowing. Phew.

Lunch at Club 55 the next day resembled the Chelsea Flower Show, except in casual dress: corporate Britain comes to the

Riviera. A member of the restaurant staff stood outside the
men's loo (55 does up to 900 covers a day but it still only has
two single urinals and one stall) putting FTSE 100 CEOs into
a holding pattern, while ladies (four cubicles) slipped past.
Our host had asked me to undertake the very important task of
transporting his bathing trunks in my beach bag; after lunch he
changed, swam and put his boxer shorts in there for me to carry
back.

The next morning I realised I still had them. All the
houseguests were assembled outside – should I present them to
him in front of the others? Should I give them to the staff (and
what would they think)? Should I try and sneak them into his
bedroom (his wife, like Mr M, had stayed in the UK)? Should I
leave them in my room for his cleaner to notice when she came
in to make my bed? Unable to face any of these options, I kept
them hidden, and then forgot about them.

On the Monday evening we flew back. Because of my own
aviation enthusiasm, I can no longer sit on private jets and just
read *Hello!* magazine. I asked questions for the entire flight:
"why is the airspeed indicator not accurate at Flight Level
410?"; "why is it mandatory to have anti-skid to land at London
City?" and so on. Back home, in front of Mr M's startled gaze,
I unpacked a pair of Gap boxer shorts, large (34-36in waist). I
had some explaining to do – but not about the colour. They were
white.

A DIFFICULT LESSON IN TOUGH LOVE
*Sep 19, 2009*
Do you keep phone numbers? I meticulously store contact
details for everyone I meet, however random, and make notes of
what they do and where I met them. My other modus operandi
when meeting people is always to try to be as polite and helpful
as possible (within reason).

Hence, I found myself giving up an hour or so earlier this year
to cast an eye over the business strategy of a small enterprise.
On meeting the people behind the business, I discovered that it
was a rehabilitation clinic, and one of the people presenting to

me was a very impressive addiction counsellor, and herself a recovering alcoholic.

And that is where I sat up and took notice, because I have a close relative who is alcohol-dependent. It is not Mr M or any of the cost centres, but it is someone very dear to me. Those of you who have someone in their family who is alcohol- or drug-dependent will know how emotionally scarring this is. You love them, you want to help, you try to help, but they are living in another world. In their world, they are not addicts; they believe that they could give up at any time. They always have an excuse. Something is always just around the corner that will fix their problems – if only they could meet the right person/get the right job/have the right amount of money, everything would be fine. Nothing and no one ever prepared me for the self-delusion of the alcoholic. Every time they say they are going to get help, your hopes rise; and invariably they end up being crushed again. When Cost Centre #1 was about 14 or so, his school sensibly invited Elizabeth Burton-Phillips to address his year group. I have never met Burton-Phillips, and I have not heard her speak, but her words that day had a powerful effect on me. She had twin boys in 1976; despite having a very privileged start in life, they became drug-dependent. The day that Burton-Phillips spoke to CC#1's year she handed them each an envelope and told them not to open it until she instructed them to. Eventually, after hearing of how her two boys had come to be drug addicts, and what it had done to their lives and their family's lives, she let them open the envelope. It contained the death certificate of one of her sons.

The other son sought treatment and is in recovery. (I am learning the language of addiction – just as with cancer you are never "cured", you are "in remission", so with addiction, you are never "recovered", you are "in recovery" even if you have been clean for many years.) Burton-Phillips has written a book about her experience, titled Mum, Can You Lend Me Twenty Quid? It reinforces the message that I have had to learn the hard way, namely that sometimes, in order to help your loved ones, you have to sever your links with them. That is, at least until they genuinely want to help themselves. And it is very tough. So that is what I eventually did – cut myself off, emotionally and financially. I just hoped that one day, when the bottom had been reached and there was nowhere left to go, my loved one would see that seeking help – serious, professional help – was a necessity.

I know this is a column that usually seeks to entertain, and there is not much amusing about having an alcoholic in the family. But I wanted to stress the importance of keeping telephone numbers. Because the day did come, just last week, when I got a call about my relative from the emergency department of a hospital. When I telephoned the young addiction counsellor who had so impressed me months before, not only was she in the vicinity of the hospital, she dropped everything and went to help. And now she has achieved what we all have tried to for so long – to help the person concerned to cut through the self-delusion and seek real help. Not entertaining this week, I am afraid, but still hopeful.

## ARCHBISHOPS AND COMEDIANS NEED NOT APPLY
*Sep 26, 2009*

The competition to find the best ideas for Mrs Moneypenny to write about in the future has yielded many entries, including one reader who said: "Mrs M should write about the sort of people she would choose to take on once it is clear that the recession is over." There are two problems with this suggestion. The first is that I am not sure if it will ever be clear that the recession is over, and the second is that, even though it is certainly not over yet, we have started hiring again.

This month has seen two new faces join our team. It had become apparent to me over the summer months that, even though the recession was still rumbling on, it would be very short-sighted to stop hiring young people and training them. Like many other businesses, we shelved our plans to hire a graduate this year. But then we changed our minds and ran some advertisements on university websites. We even approached one or two recruitment companies that we knew and told them what kind of person we were looking for.

This was all very last-minute. My ideal way of employing someone is to have them work for us for at least one if not two university holidays before they graduate, which has proved a good way of teaching them what we do (and why it is so fascinating) and also teaching us what they are like. Our sole graduate hire in 2008, who came to us from Edinburgh University, worked her way up via this route. But this year we had to resort instead to some swift recruitment activity.

As it turned out, we took on not one but three graduates: two of them into permanent jobs and one, who is off to do a Master's later this month, for a two-week project to compile a new Mrs Moneypenny book. One came from the ad, one from a recruitment agency and one from word of mouth. Which universities? Another from Edinburgh, one from St Andrews and one from University College London.

We don't employ anyone who went to Oxford or Cambridge. (Actually, that is not strictly true – one of our team went to Oxford for a week, decided it was not for her and sought refuge at Bristol). This is not deliberate bias – it's just the way things turned out – but as a result, I don't rub shoulders with Oxbridge graduates on a daily basis.

I do rub shoulders, or at least bylines, with Richard McCann (whose mother was the first victim of Peter Sutcliffe, the Yorkshire Ripper), Aasia Mahmood (who grew up in Pakistan and has lived in Scotland for the past 24 years, working as a bilingual support teacher) and am within byline-rubbing distance of Jimmy Carr, the comedian. We are all contributors to Grandparents, a new anthology of articles on that subject co-edited by Sarah Brown, our PM's wife. At a tea party to launch the book, I met Carr and like a starstruck teenager asked him to sign my copy.

Cost Centre #1 and I saw Carr for the first time in 2002, in a show entitled Bare-Faced Ambition, at the Edinburgh Fringe. It was a small venue, and Carr noticed CC#1 walk in with me and showed theatrical concern over the suitability of his show for a boy of 12.

These days Carr plays much bigger venues, including City Hall, Newcastle, where he will be appearing at the end of October. CC#1 is off to Newcastle University this month and will turn 20 on October 31, so a ticket to Carr's show seems a good birthday idea. I will still be basking in my new-found "I'm in a book with Jimmy Carr" street cred and trying to ignore the fact that he is on page 40 while I am a lot further in. Still, the Archbishop of Canterbury is even further in. As you can tell, I am delighted to be in such exalted company – although since both Carr and the Archbishop are Cambridge graduates, I probably wouldn't hire them even if the recession were over.

## SUPPER WITH THE SUPERMODELS IN NEW YORK CITY
*Oct 2, 2009*

Who is that? At a large dinner in New York City I felt somewhat disadvantaged since I couldn't identify most of the people in the room . And if I could, it wasn't because I had met them. I did, for instance, recognise Nicole Kidman, who was sitting next to Her Majesty Queen Rania of Jordan. But they were only two and there were more than 300 women gathered as guests of Indra Nooyi, Wendi Murdoch and Queen Rania at the fourth Important Dinner for Women in support of Millennium Development Goal Five, the reduction of maternal mortality.

Most of us were mothers, and we were there to pledge our resources (time, money, talent) to ensuring that fewer women die in childbirth in the developing world. While all three of our hosts spoke, it was Sarah Brown, wife of the Prime Minister, who issued the call to arms. One woman after another stood up and pledged to help, including quite a few Brits (Naomi Campbell and Geri Halliwell, for example, and yes, I did know who they were). I was sitting between two women whose husbands worked in the music industry, and they were brilliant at helping me out when, yet again, I didn't recognise someone.

I had to be told by the lady on my left who Gayle King was, after she stopped by our table to say hello, and then when Diana Taylor stood up to chair the open-mike session, the lady on my right had to explain that she dated Michael Bloomberg, the Mayor of New York. I never realised dinner companions could be so useful. If it were up to me, I would take those two with me to all major social events that I attend.

Sadly for me, they are not available for general briefing duties; one is married to Bono and the other to David Bowie. Iman told me that she has two children, a nine-year-old with Bowie and a 30-year-old from a previous relationship. A 30-year-old? I knew I should have taken my hearing aid. I asked her to repeat it twice, I was so incredulous. "I'm 54," this vision of perfection announced, producing her reading glasses from her handbag to prove it.

Presumably as part of an orchestrated campaign to make me feel inadequate, I was on the "former supermodels" table, with Helena Christensen and Christy Turlington. The latter I had seen praised earlier in the day during a session on maternal health at the United Nations by no less a person than the Prime Minister of Tanzania, not someone I was aware was familiar with former supermodels. But Turlington, who is a mother of two young children and studying for a masters in public health at Columbia, showed a short and powerful film at the UN session, some of which had been shot (with considerable difficulty) in Tanzania. That's the kind of achievement that makes me feel much more inadequate than simply being about three times her body mass.

Current supermodels were on other tables; Natalia Vodianova is so tall that I needed her to sit down before I could appreciate quite how beautiful this Russian model turned wife, mother and philanthropist is. But the role model that I was longing to meet, and never quite managed to, was Pulitzer-prize-winning author Sheryl WuDunn, whose book *Half the Sky* I had read on the plane on the way over. I recommend it despite its sobering subtitle, *Turning Oppression into Opportunity for Women Worldwide*; it is both inspiring and educative.

I can say the same of my dinner companions. I am not easily intimidated, but place me between Ali Hewson and Iman for two hours or so and I get nervous. Both are older than me and look years younger (Hewson has extraordinary natural beauty, and on a table of supermodels held her own) and both were very welcoming to an overweight middle-aged mother-of-three who hadn't a clue who anyone was.

## LAY OFF BANKERS' BONUSES – THEY'LL HELP PAY BACK THE BUDGET DEFECIT

*Oct 10, 2009*

Are bonuses a bad thing? Much of the debate about how to avert another financial crisis has centred on them. This misses the point. Lehman, the highest-profile failure, paid a large portion of its staff remuneration in shares that they could only get their hands on over a period of years. This seems to be close to what most people are proposing now. Yet it didn't stop Lehman collapsing.

I don't believe it is the structure of bankers' pay deals that everyone is getting worked up about. I suspect it is their sheer size. That is nothing more than envy, which does not require legislation. If people have difficulty with bankers earning such large sums, they need to stop banks from making the kind of profits that enable those bonuses to be paid. Is that practical? Is it desirable? Should governments interfere with markets? I don't think so.

Blaming bonuses for everything is as flawed as it is convenient. Among those who refuse to see bonuses as the root of all evil is the chairman of the Financial Services Authority, Adair Turner. "It is possible," he recently argued in a speech at the Mansion House in the City of London "to overstate the importance of bonus structures in the origins of the crisis: they were, I believe, much less important than huge failures in capital adequacy and liquidity regulation."

The super-normal profits that investment banks make come about partly because (whatever people say) the City is not a perfectly efficient market. Companies don't – indeed can't – shop around for advice or underwriting services. To use a recent example, can you imagine Liberty International's finance director calling every investment bank in town to ask: "Right, how much would you quote me for an accelerated book building process to place 9.9 per cent of our issued capital?" If he had, the secret would have been out and the deal (or at least, its pricing) dead in the water. When Merrill Lynch agreed a price with him, I doubt they did so in competition with three of four other suppliers.

Companies are not indifferent over who advises them or places their shares, any more than I am indifferent over who cuts my hair. I am not going to call around to find the best price for a haircut or colour – it would take too long and in any case I wouldn't trust most of the candidates to do it right. The best hairdressers, my own included, charge very handsomely for their services and keep a substantial proportion of their fee as incentive pay – tips. They do not have ceilings imposed on their compensation, they do not receive deferred payments and their employers are free to compete on price or any other basis in what, like banking, is an imperfect market. Like investment banks, they may come up with products and services that are "socially irrelevant", to quote Lord Turner again.

But even social irrelevance is ultimately a matter of opinion. Lord Turner may not want to go out on a Saturday and buy a Collateralised Debt Obligation-squared, but equally he may not wish to get his hair done in such a way that he does not have to blow-dry it for 12 weeks. (Adair, just in case this does appeal, I suggest Urban Retreat at Harrods. It's called a Brazilian and costs about £300, and I am desperate to find the time to go and get it done.)

So, please lay off bankers. Let's admit that our only problem with the way they are paid is that some of us are jealous that we don't earn that much ourselves. And let's get back to focusing on solutions more likely to help, such as whether we need a new Glass-Steagall Act, or something like it, that would help to prevent riskier businesses from endangering safer ones. Just consider this – if bankers are not receiving bonuses and paying tax on them, where is the money going to come from to pay back our horrendous budget deficit?

## NANO-CANAPÉS (AND NO FIZZ) WITH THE TORY PARTY PEOPLE
*Oct 17, 2009*
Bethlehem, by comparison, would have seemed positively spacious. If you ever needed confirmation that Britain expects

its next government to be formed by David Cameron, you should have been in Manchester in early October. Even if you could have found one, a stable would have been charging several hundred pounds a night – with straw extra.
I confess that I was, until this month, a political party conference virgin. I have never seen the point of filling in (months in advance) lots of forms that require everything from my National Insurance number to my blood type, and then going to a place where lots of worthy types stand around discussing the finer points of policies that are unlikely to see the light of day.

But times change, and small business owners need to get closer to the people who will probably form the next government. I was not alone. Even my Media Entrepreneur Girlfriend, the daughter of a famous Marxist historian and so not a likely visitor to Manchester, turned up. MEG did look a little sheepish, as though she expected her family or her former classmates at Camden High School for Girls to jump out from behind a plant in the Midland Hotel and shout "traitor!" But she went with the flow and lingered in fringe sessions listening to shadow cabinet members.

I am encouraged by the ideas that Cameron & Co are suggesting for small businesses. A lower rate of corporation tax is to be encouraged, as is an automatic right to business rate relief for smaller companies. The Conservatives seem to have woken up to the fact that the vast majority of businesses in the UK (and by that, I mean more than 90 per cent) employ fewer than 250 people.

I had expected it would be busy. I had expected that the food would be expensive. I was not even surprised to queue for my lunch in the conference hall and then find I had to sit on the floor to eat it. But I was not prepared for the canapé pricing strategy of the conference caterers. This year, my business has been represented at all three main party conferences. At each, we have sponsored a fringe event, hosted by the employment charity Tomorrow's People, on the subject of intergenerational joblessness. (In Manchester, I leafleted delegates to drum up attendance, a humbling experience as people rushed past, averting their gaze.)

As is customary at these events, we provided refreshments. (Not champagne. Our prospective Prime Minister had decreed that he didn't wish to see his senior team members standing around drinking fizz, so we served some pretty average wine at £18.50 a bottle.) But we had ordered canapés, for 30 people, at £10 a head.

All £300 of it turned up on one smallish serving dish. Each canapé was about 2cm square at most. And each one cost more than £3. I needed something stronger than my reading glasses (1.5x) just to see them. Forget eating them, I suggested that we frame them – on a surface-area basis they were more valuable than anything Damien Hirst has produced. Even better, let's put them in the Bank of England to help make up for the gold that our current Prime Minister sold off when he was Chancellor of the Exchequer.

As the conference caterers discovered, serving inadequate and overpriced canapés to guests of Mrs Moneypenny is something you do at your peril. I chewed up and spat out not the food, but the poor catering manger assigned to our fringe event, despite his perfectly valid assertion that this was all we had ordered. In future, I shall insist on seeing a life-size photograph of what I am buying. Extra food was produced, but the level of under-catering combined with a very popular event (Theresa May spoke and, for once, no one was worrying about her footwear) meant that we had a challenge on our hands.

Forget Bethlehem. It was more a case of loaves and fishes.

## WHAT EVERY TEENAGER REALLY, REALLY WANTS TO KNOW
*Oct 24, 2009*

What is happening in Armenia? No, I don't need an answer, I listen to Radio 4 every day so I am fully briefed on protests in Armenia just as I am on the gubernatorial race in Texas and which butterflies have recently become extinct in England. Just as well, since Armenia was the first question of the day from Cost Centre #2 last week when I took him to catch the school bus.

We are now a dayboy house. This might be the norm for most families, but given my previous habit of outsourcing the Cost Centres to boarding school almost as soon as they could walk, it is a big culture shock, and not just because I have to answer questions on Armenia. (CC#3 catches the bus from down the road and on a nice day walks to school, so I don't have to cope with his interrogations which are at any rate much less challenging and more to do with the Premier League, about which, I might add, I know even less than I do about Armenia.)

Readers have written in and asked how the CCs (or the Reduced CCs) are getting on in their new schools. Very well, thank you, which is more than can be said for me. CC#2 recently turned 15, inconveniently on a Wednesday. When children are at boarding school, midweek birthdays are easy. Send a card, and then a text and an e-mail, book a birthday cake to be delivered at tea, and plan something special for the following weekend. I was not prepared for a day school child's midweek birthday.

For a start, I managed to book CC#2's latest orthodontic appointment on his birthday. So on the day he turned 15 he spent half an hour or so in a surgery in Oxford having his teeth photographed and impressions taken ready for the braces that will be in place by Christmas. Personally, I don't think that CC#2 needs braces, but he disagrees. And while it might have been an administrative error, once I learned how much they were going to cost I thought that his braces would serve very well as a birthday present – and Christmas present, and next year's birthday and so on for at least five years.

But then I realised that he would not be home until quite late and I too would only just have got home – with no energy for birthday celebrations. So I called on the services of my Medical Girlfriend, who has never sent any of her three children to boarding school and who lives in Oxford, handily near the orthodontist. Could I, I begged in an e-mail, outsource the birthday to her?

MG came to the rescue. She provided pizza, salad, cake, beer and wine (these last needed for Mr M, who had learned by e-mail at the 11th hour that he had to drive to Oxford for the evening), and above all the company of her soon-to-be 15-year-old daughter. This girl shows great promise – "I have given CC#2 a birthday present," she announced. "I have given him my telephone number."

It was probably the best birthday present a 15-year-old boy could hope for, although I am sure her mother would have an opinion on any fraternisation. I vividly remember when we were a lot, lot younger and MG had her home and her practice in a leafy street in London SW3 at the time. We both had one son. Hers had a large playroom with a well-stocked toy cupboard that my CC#1 used to trash until he was banned by MG from going round there to play. I have counselled CC#2 not to make a mess anywhere or he may suffer the same fate.

Birthdays aside, it is very handy having a teenaged son at home. He has turned his hand to tasks as varied as helping me rehearse for my radio telephony exam ("Golf Oscar November," intoned the newly lowered voice over the kitchen table, "pass your message") and changing the sheets. "Mum," he said as we struggled with the duvet cover late one evening, "what is it like to be married for more than 20 years?" I think we'll stick to Armenia.

## WHY MY SHOOTING DAYS ARE ALL IN A NOBEL CAUSE
*Oct 30, 2009*
The Nobel judges got it spot on this year, I reckon. I have been waiting for them to honour someone sensible even if – yet again – it's an American. Have you noticed how many Nobel laureates come from the US? But let's not begrudge the man his award. It was well deserved. Mind you, from the press coverage, you would never have guessed so.

I am talking about Oliver Williamson, this year's winner of the Economics prize, for "his analysis of economic governance, especially the boundaries of the firm". (Ha! Got you there.) I was excited to read that Williamson had won because not only is he something of a hero of mine (and extensively quoted in my PhD thesis) but also because the article in which I learnt of his honour did not mention it until the very end.

Acres of coverage, instead, went to the woman who had shared
the prize with him, Elinor Ostrom. This seemed to be on the
pretext that she was worth three times as many column inches
as him because she was the first woman to win it. So? I have
never heard of her, and Williamson I quote all the time, even
(and this may have been a first for him) in an article I wrote
about lapdancing for a Sunday newspaper three weeks ago. He
turned 77 the other day – what a great birthday present. (The
Nobel Prize, that is, not the mention in my article.)

Strictly speaking the Nobel Prize for Economics is no such
thing. It was not one of the five prizes established under the
terms of Alfred Nobel's will. The Sveriges riksbanks pris i
ekonomisk vetenskap till Alfred Nobels minne, or Sveriges
Riksbank Prize in Economic Sciences in Memory of Alfred
Nobel, was set up in 1968 (72 years after Alfred went to join his
maker) by the Swedish Central Bank, which was looking for a
suitable way to mark the 300th anniversary of its establishment.
Since there are almost 300 words in the name of the prize, it
must have seemed spot on. (This, by the way, was the first and
last time that the Nobel Foundation allowed anyone else to join
in. It's probably just as well. What next? The Abba Music Prize
in memory of Alfred Nobel? The Ikea Design Prize in memory
of Alfred Nobel? A procession of Swedish organisations
inventing Nobel prizes is probably not a great idea.)

To make it look like a "proper" Nobel prize, laureates in
economics are selected by the Royal Swedish Academy of
Sciences, as are the laureates in chemistry and physics, and they
get roughly the same amount of money (SKr10m, £909,000). I
wonder what Williamson will do with his. At 77, he presumably
has plenty of time for shopping. Indeed, his website says that
his office hours are 3pm-4pm every Thursday. (I wish mine
were!)

My all-time favourite Williamson article is 30 years old this
month. "Transaction Cost Economics: The Governance of
Contractual Relations" was published in the Journal of Law
and Economics in October 1979. For those with little time to
spare (in which case you should avoid reading Willamson's CV,
which even before his Nobel prize ran to 36 pages), I will sum

up his theory for you: trust lowers transaction costs. In other words, if I know and trust you, it will cost me less money to do business with you, and therefore I am more likely to do so.

Oliver, your paper was very influential and is the reason why I work a four-day week at this time of the year. By regularly spending 24 hours a week in the countryside killing birds alongside captains of industry, I am able to get to know them and so build valuable relationships, thereby creating trust and lowering transaction costs. So, when you collect your prize in Stockholm on December 10 (which, by the way, is the last day of the grouse-shooting season here in the UK), please know that there is a small business owner in London who will be applauding like mad – which is no more than you deserve.

## NOW YOU ARE ALL IN DANGER OF A FLYING VISIT
*Nov 06, 2009*

"Is that wise?" Life has become so hectic that the only way I seem able to communicate with Mr M between 07.00 and 21.00 every day is by e-mail. This particular inquiry came during an exchange that had started with me telling him that we were going to take Cost Centre #1 out for lunch on his 20th birthday. In Newcastle upon Tyne.

"Are we going by train or car?" e-mailed Mr M in reply. Neither, I wrote back. We are going by plane. Piloted by me. I am delighted to tell you that I am now a qualified PPL(A) and can take passengers along with me as I cruise the skies of central England. Newcastle upon Tyne is 255 miles from Oxford as the crow flies, and also as I fly. In a little Piper PA28 at about 95 knots it is therefore more than two hours away. But how fabulous to be able to go up for lunch, looking down at everywhere on the way, and then come home again in time for dinner! The poor boy will soon be living in dread of his mother turning up at the drop of a hat.

For the one or two of you who have written to condemn me for continuing to fly and suggesting I should be spending the money on school fees instead, let me assure you that if I could have kept everyone in school by giving up flying, I would have. But the whole exercise, which has taken from March 2008

149

to October 2009, interrupted by a poor August in '08 and an equally useless July in '09, has cost less than one term's school fees for one child. That is not a measure of how cheap it is to learn to fly, it is a measure of how ridiculously expensive our schools have become in the UK.

The final three days of my journey towards qualifying as a pilot saw me take my radio telephony exam, my final written exam and then my skills test. I was not surprised that I passed the written exam, Flight Planning and Performance. Most of it is physics and about doing balance/mass calculations: how does the centre of gravity of an aircraft move if you fly for three hours and use up lots of fuel, and so on. In practice, with me at the controls, the answer is straightforward – I weigh so much more than the average female pilot that the aircraft's centre of gravity doesn't move much at all. But exams are not real life – all women pilots wear a size 10 dress as far as I can see.

Before I submitted my paperwork to the Civil Aviation Authority I bought a new logbook and copied out my original one, which was, I am ashamed to say, a little scruffy. One pilot with an immaculately completed logbook was Sir Keith Park, who even while directing the Battle of Britain and flying around airfields in the summer of 1940 filled his in meticulously. For those of you lucky enough to have been at the unveiling of his statue on Wednesday last, you will have seen a facsimile of a 1940 page from his logbook in the programme. The journey from the idea first mooted in this column in September 2007, that there should be a proper memorial to him in Trafalgar Square, to the arrival of his likeness on the Fourth Plinth, has taken a little longer than my pilot training, but not much. And as both things show, where there is determination, and a lot of support, it is possible to accomplish what might have seemed impossible.

I am sad that I never met Sir Keith Park. But I do know that had I told him that I planned to fly to Newcastle upon Tyne, he would have been very unlikely to reply: "Is that wise?"

PS. As well as celebrating my new-found status as a pilot, I am also sending out bottles of Krug to the three winners of my reader competition a few weeks ago: Anthony Robson, Sharifah

Also available from Masterley Publishing

**The Best of Alex 1998 - 2001**

**The Best of Alex 2002**

**The Best of Alex 20**

**The Best of Alex 2004**

**The Best of Alex 2005**

**The Best of Alex 200**

**The Best of Alex 2007**

**The Best of Alex 2008**

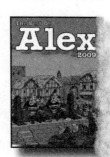

**The Best of Alex 20**

**Mrs Moneypenny Returns**

**Celeb**

Amirah and Angela Woodburn. And an honourable mention to
Alexandra Wilson ("cost centres are people too") who prefers
alcopops to Krug. Thank you everyone who wrote in.